MW01010934

THIS PLANNER BELONGS TO:

_____

_____

_____

_____

Index

(C) MOTHERLY LOVE PRESS   ALL RIGHTS RESERVED

NO PART OF THIS BOOK MAY BE REPRODUCED, DISTRIBUTED OR TRANSMITTED IN
ANY FORM OR BY ANY MEANS; INCLUDING PHOTOCOPYING, RECORDING OR OTHER
ELECTRONIC OR MECHANICAL METHODS WITHOUT PRIOR WRITTEN PERMISSION OF THE
PUBLISHER/AUTHOR.

motherly
love
press

JULY

- [ ] _____
- [ ] _____
- [ ] _____
- [ ] _____
- [ ] _____
- [ ] _____
- [ ] _____
- [ ] _____

AUGUST

- [ ] _____
- [ ] _____
- [ ] _____
- [ ] _____
- [ ] _____
- [ ] _____
- [ ] _____
- [ ] _____

SEPTEMBER

- [ ] _____
- [ ] _____
- [ ] _____
- [ ] _____
- [ ] _____
- [ ] _____
- [ ] _____
- [ ] _____

OCTOBER

- [ ] _____
- [ ] _____
- [ ] _____
- [ ] _____
- [ ] _____
- [ ] _____
- [ ] _____
- [ ] _____

NOVEMBER

- [ ] _____
- [ ] _____
- [ ] _____
- [ ] _____
- [ ] _____
- [ ] _____
- [ ] _____
- [ ] _____

DECEMBER

- [ ] _____
- [ ] _____
- [ ] _____
- [ ] _____
- [ ] _____
- [ ] _____
- [ ] _____
- [ ] _____

JANUARY

- [ ] _____
- [ ] _____
- [ ] _____
- [ ] _____
- [ ] _____
- [ ] _____
- [ ] _____
- [ ] _____

FEBRUARY

- [ ] _____
- [ ] _____
- [ ] _____
- [ ] _____
- [ ] _____
- [ ] _____
- [ ] _____
- [ ] _____

MARCH

- [ ] _____
- [ ] _____
- [ ] _____
- [ ] _____
- [ ] _____
- [ ] _____
- [ ] _____
- [ ] _____

APRIL

- [ ] _____
- [ ] _____
- [ ] _____
- [ ] _____
- [ ] _____
- [ ] _____
- [ ] _____
- [ ] _____

MAY

- [ ] _____
- [ ] _____
- [ ] _____
- [ ] _____
- [ ] _____
- [ ] _____
- [ ] _____
- [ ] _____

JUNE

- [ ] _____
- [ ] _____
- [ ] _____
- [ ] _____
- [ ] _____
- [ ] _____
- [ ] _____
- [ ] _____

2024-2025
YEAR-AT-A-GLANCE

JULY

S	M	T	W	T	F	S
	1	2	3	4	5	6
7	8	9	10	11	12	13
14	15	16	17	18	19	20
21	22	23	24	25	26	27
28	29	30	31			

AUGUST

S	M	T	W	T	F	S
				1	2	3
4	5	6	7	8	9	10
11	12	13	14	15	16	17
18	19	20	21	22	23	24
25	26	27	28	29	30	31

SEPTEMBER

S	M	T	W	T	F	S
1	2	3	4	5	6	7
8	9	10	11	12	13	14
15	16	17	18	19	20	21
22	23	24	25	26	27	28
29	30					

OCTOBER

S	M	T	W	T	F	S
		1	2	3	4	5
6	7	8	9	10	11	12
13	14	15	16	17	18	19
20	21	22	23	24	25	26
27	28	29	30	31		

NOVEMBER

S	M	T	W	T	F	S
					1	2
3	4	5	6	7	8	9
10	11	12	13	14	15	16
17	18	19	20	21	22	23
24	25	26	27	28	29	30

DECEMBER

S	M	T	W	T	F	S
1	2	3	4	5	6	7
8	9	10	11	12	13	14
15	16	17	18	19	20	21
22	23	24	25	26	27	28
29	30	31				

JANUARY

S	M	T	W	T	F	S
			1	2	3	4
5	6	7	8	9	10	11
12	13	14	15	16	17	18
19	20	21	22	23	24	25
26	27	28	29	30	31	

FEBRUARY

S	M	T	W	T	F	S
						1
2	3	4	5	6	7	8
9	10	11	12	13	14	15
16	17	18	19	20	21	22
23	24	25	26	27	28	

MARCH

S	M	T	W	T	F	S
						1
2	3	4	5	6	7	8
9	10	11	12	13	14	15
16	17	18	19	20	21	22
23	24	25	26	27	28	29
30	31					

APRIL

S	M	T	W	T	F	S
		1	2	3	4	5
6	7	8	9	10	11	12
13	14	15	16	17	18	19
20	21	22	23	24	25	26
27	28	29	30			

MAY

S	M	T	W	T	F	S
				1	2	3
4	5	6	7	8	9	10
11	12	13	14	15	16	17
18	19	20	21	22	23	24
25	26	27	28	29	30	31

JUNE

S	M	T	W	T	F	S
1	2	3	4	5	6	7
8	9	10	11	12	13	14
15	16	17	18	19	20	21
22	23	24	25	26	27	28
29	30					

School Routine

Time	
7:00 am	
7:30 am	
8:00 am	
8:30 am	
9:00 am	
9:30 am	
10:00 am	
10:30 am	
11:00 am	
11:30 am	
12:00 pm	
12:30 pm	
1:00 pm	
1:30 pm	
2:00 pm	
2:30 pm	
3:00 pm	
3:30 pm	
4:00 pm	
4:30 pm	
5:00 pm	
5:30 pm	
6:00 pm	
6:30 pm	
7:00 pm	
7:30 pm	
8:00 pm	
8:30 pm	

Notes for the Substitute

Teaching kids to count is fine,
but teaching kids what counts
is best.

———————

Bob Talbert

Attendance

NAME:

Learning never exhausts
the mind

Leonardo de Vinci

	JULY	AUGUST	SEPTEMBER	OCTOBER	NOVEMBER	DECEMBER	JANUARY	FEBRUARY	MARCH	APRIL	MAY	JUNE
1												
2												
3												
4												
5												
6												
7												
8												
9												
10												
11												
12												
13												
14												
15												
16												
17												
18												
19												
20												
21												
22												
23												
24												
25												
26												
27												
28												
29									■				
30									■				
31			■		■				■		■		■

Grade Report

NAME: _____

GRADE: _____

SUBJECTS	Week 1	Week 2	Week 3	Week 4	Week 5	Week 6	Week 7	Week 8	Week 9	Week 10	Week 11	Week 12	Week 13	Week 14	Week 15	Week 16	Week 17	Week 18

An investment in knowledge pays the best interest.

Benjamin Franklin

SUBJECTS	Week 19	Week 20	Week 21	Week 22	Week 23	Week 24	Week 25	Week 26	Week 27	Week 28	Week 29	Week 30	Week 31	Week 32	Week 33	Week 34	Week 35	Week 36

That's the thing about books, they let you travel without moving your feet.

_____

Jhumpa Lahiri

Reading Log   NAME: _____

Date	Title/Author	Minutes Read	Parent Initials

The best way to find yourself is to lose yourself in the service of others

———————————

Mahatma Gandi

Community Service

NAME: _____

Date	Organization Served	Time Spent	Notes

Field Trip Itinerary

DATE: _____

Location: _____

Address: _____

Contact: _____

Arrival Time: _____

Departure Time: _____

Educational Goals:

_____
_____
_____
_____
_____
_____
_____

Takeaways:

_____
_____
_____
_____
_____
_____

Field Trip Itinerary

DATE: _____

Location: _____

Address: _____

Contact: _____

Arrival Time: _____

Departure Time: _____

Educational Goals:

_____
_____
_____
_____
_____
_____
_____

Takeaways:

_____
_____
_____
_____
_____
_____
_____

Field Trip Itinerary

DATE: _____

Location: _____

Address: _____

Contact: _____

Arrival Time: _____

Departure Time: _____

Educational Goals:

_____
_____
_____
_____
_____
_____
_____
_____

Takeaways:

_____
_____
_____
_____
_____
_____
_____

Field Trip Itinerary

DATE: _____

Location: _____
Address: _____
Contact: _____
Arrival Time: _____
Departure Time: _____

Educational Goals:

_____
_____
_____
_____
_____
_____
_____

Takeaways:

_____
_____
_____
_____
_____
_____
_____

Field Trip Itinerary

DATE: _____

Location: _____

Address: _____

Contact: _____

Arrival Time: _____

Departure Time: _____

Educational Goals:

_____
_____
_____
_____
_____
_____
_____

Takeaways:

_____
_____
_____
_____
_____
_____

Field Trip Itinerary

DATE: _____

Location: _____
Address: _____
Contact: _____
Arrival Time: _____
Departure Time: _____

Educational Goals:

_____
_____
_____
_____
_____
_____
_____

Takeaways:

_____
_____
_____
_____
_____
_____
_____

Field Trip Itinerary

DATE: _____

Location: _____

Address: _____

Contact: _____

Arrival Time: _____

Departure Time: _____

Educational Goals:

_____
_____
_____
_____
_____
_____
_____

Takeaways:

_____
_____
_____
_____
_____
_____

Field Trip Itinerary

DATE: _____

Location: _____

Address: _____

Contact: _____

Arrival Time: _____

Departure Time: _____

Educational Goals:

_____

_____

_____

_____

_____

_____

_____

Takeaways:

_____

_____

_____

_____

_____

_____

_____

July 2024

SUNDAY	MONDAY	TUESDAY	WEDNESDAY
	1	2	3
7	8	9	10
14	15	16	17
21	22	23	24
28	29	30	31

July 2024

THURSDAY	FRIDAY	SATURDAY	NOTES
4	5	6	
11	12	13	
18	19	20	
25	26	27	

	SUNDAY	MONDAY	TUESDAY	WEDNESDAY
	SUNDAY	MONDAY	TUESDAY	WEDNESDAY

Jun - Jul LESSON PLANS Week of 30th - 6th

THURSDAY	FRIDAY	SATURDAY

Weekly Supplies

- ☐ _____
- ☐ _____
- ☐ _____
- ☐ _____
- ☐ _____
- ☐ _____
- ☐ _____
- ☐ _____
- ☐ _____
- ☐ _____
- ☐ _____
- ☐ _____

To Dos

- ☐ _____
- ☐ _____
- ☐ _____
- ☐ _____
- ☐ _____
- ☐ _____
- ☐ _____
- ☐ _____
- ☐ _____
- ☐ _____
- ☐ _____

Notes

- ☐ _____
- ☐ _____
- ☐ _____
- ☐ _____
- ☐ _____
- ☐ _____
- ☐ _____
- ☐ _____
- ☐ _____

Weekly Schedule

	SUNDAY	MONDAY	TUESDAY
7:00 am			
7:30 am			
8:00 am			
8:30 am			
9:00 am			
9:30 am			
10:00 am			
10:30 am			
11:00 am			
11:30 am			
12:00 pm			
12:30 pm			
1:00 pm			
1:30 pm			
2:00 pm			
2:30 pm			
3:00 pm			
3:30 pm			
4:00 pm			
4:30 pm			
5:00 pm			
5:30 pm			
6:00 pm			
6:30 pm			
7:00 pm			
7:30 pm			
8:00 pm			
8:30 pm			

Jun - Jul

Week of 30th - 6th

	WEDNESDAY	THURSDAY	FRIDAY	SATURDAY
7:00 am				
7:30 am				
8:00 am				
8:30 am				
9:00 am				
9:30 am				
10:00 am				
10:30 am				
11:00 am				
11:30 am				
12:00 pm				
12:30 pm				
1:00 pm				
1:30 pm				
2:00 pm				
2:30 pm				
3:00 pm				
3:30 pm				
4:00 pm				
4:30 pm				
5:00 pm				
5:30 pm				
6:00 pm				
6:30 pm				
7:00 pm				
7:30 pm				
8:00 pm				
8:30 pm				

	SUNDAY	MONDAY	TUESDAY	WEDNESDAY

July LESSON PLANS Week of 7th - 13th

THURSDAY	FRIDAY	SATURDAY

Weekly Supplies

- ☐ _____
- ☐ _____
- ☐ _____
- ☐ _____
- ☐ _____
- ☐ _____
- ☐ _____
- ☐ _____
- ☐ _____
- ☐ _____
- ☐ _____
- ☐ _____

To Dos

- ☐ _____
- ☐ _____
- ☐ _____
- ☐ _____
- ☐ _____
- ☐ _____
- ☐ _____
- ☐ _____
- ☐ _____
- ☐ _____
- ☐ _____
- ☐ _____

Notes

- ☐ _____
- ☐ _____
- ☐ _____
- ☐ _____
- ☐ _____
- ☐ _____
- ☐ _____
- ☐ _____
- ☐ _____

Weekly Schedule

	SUNDAY	MONDAY	TUESDAY
7:00 am			
7:30 am			
8:00 am			
8:30 am			
9:00 am			
9:30 am			
10:00 am			
10:30 am			
11:00 am			
11:30 am			
12:00 pm			
12:30 pm			
1:00 pm			
1:30 pm			
2:00 pm			
2:30 pm			
3:00 pm			
3:30 pm			
4:00 pm			
4:30 pm			
5:00 pm			
5:30 pm			
6:00 pm			
6:30 pm			
7:00 pm			
7:30 pm			
8:00 pm			
8:30 pm			

July

Week of 7th - 13th

	WEDNESDAY	THURSDAY	FRIDAY	SATURDAY
7:00 am				
7:30 am				
8:00 am				
8:30 am				
9:00 am				
9:30 am				
10:00 am				
10:30 am				
11:00 am				
11:30 am				
12:00 pm				
12:30 pm				
1:00 pm				
1:30 pm				
2:00 pm				
2:30 pm				
3:00 pm				
3:30 pm				
4:00 pm				
4:30 pm				
5:00 pm				
5:30 pm				
6:00 pm				
6:30 pm				
7:00 pm				
7:30 pm				
8:00 pm				
8:30 pm				

	SUNDAY	MONDAY	TUESDAY	WEDNESDAY
	SUNDAY	MONDAY	TUESDAY	WEDNESDAY

July LESSON PLANS Week of 14th - 20th

THURSDAY	FRIDAY	SATURDAY

- [ ] _____
- [ ] _____
- [ ] _____
- [ ] _____
- [ ] _____
- [ ] _____
- [ ] _____
- [ ] _____
- [ ] _____
- [ ] _____
- [ ] _____
- [ ] _____

To Dos

- [ ] _____
- [ ] _____
- [ ] _____
- [ ] _____
- [ ] _____
- [ ] _____
- [ ] _____
- [ ] _____
- [ ] _____
- [ ] _____
- [ ] _____

Notes

- [ ] _____
- [ ] _____
- [ ] _____
- [ ] _____
- [ ] _____
- [ ] _____
- [ ] _____
- [ ] _____
- [ ] _____

Weekly Schedule

	SUNDAY	MONDAY	TUESDAY
7:00 am			
7:30 am			
8:00 am			
8:30 am			
9:00 am			
9:30 am			
10:00 am			
10:30 am			
11:00 am			
11:30 am			
12:00 pm			
12:30 pm			
1:00 pm			
1:30 pm			
2:00 pm			
2:30 pm			
3:00 pm			
3:30 pm			
4:00 pm			
4:30 pm			
5:00 pm			
5:30 pm			
6:00 pm			
6:30 pm			
7:00 pm			
7:30 pm			
8:00 pm			
8:30 pm			

July

Week of 14th - 20th

	WEDNESDAY	THURSDAY	FRIDAY	SATURDAY
7:00 am				
7:30 am				
8:00 am				
8:30 am				
9:00 am				
9:30 am				
10:00 am				
10:30 am				
11:00 am				
11:30 am				
12:00 pm				
12:30 pm				
1:00 pm				
1:30 pm				
2:00 pm				
2:30 pm				
3:00 pm				
3:30 pm				
4:00 pm				
4:30 pm				
5:00 pm				
5:30 pm				
6:00 pm				
6:30 pm				
7:00 pm				
7:30 pm				
8:00 pm				
8:30 pm				

	SUNDAY	MONDAY	TUESDAY	WEDNESDAY

July   LESSON PLANS   Week of 21st - 27th

THURSDAY	FRIDAY	SATURDAY

Weekly Supplies

- [ ] _____
- [ ] _____
- [ ] _____
- [ ] _____
- [ ] _____
- [ ] _____
- [ ] _____
- [ ] _____
- [ ] _____
- [ ] _____
- [ ] _____
- [ ] _____

To Dos

- [ ] _____
- [ ] _____
- [ ] _____
- [ ] _____
- [ ] _____
- [ ] _____
- [ ] _____
- [ ] _____
- [ ] _____
- [ ] _____
- [ ] _____
- [ ] _____

Notes

- [ ] _____
- [ ] _____
- [ ] _____
- [ ] _____
- [ ] _____
- [ ] _____
- [ ] _____
- [ ] _____
- [ ] _____

Weekly Schedule

	SUNDAY	MONDAY	TUESDAY
7:00 am			
7:30 am			
8:00 am			
8:30 am			
9:00 am			
9:30 am			
10:00 am			
10:30 am			
11:00 am			
11:30 am			
12:00 pm			
12:30 pm			
1:00 pm			
1:30 pm			
2:00 pm			
2:30 pm			
3:00 pm			
3:30 pm			
4:00 pm			
4:30 pm			
5:00 pm			
5:30 pm			
6:00 pm			
6:30 pm			
7:00 pm			
7:30 pm			
8:00 pm			
8:30 pm			

July

Week of 21st - 27th

	WEDNESDAY	THURSDAY	FRIDAY	SATURDAY
7:00 am				
7:30 am				
8:00 am				
8:30 am				
9:00 am				
9:30 am				
10:00 am				
10:30 am				
11:00 am				
11:30 am				
12:00 pm				
12:30 pm				
1:00 pm				
1:30 pm				
2:00 pm				
2:30 pm				
3:00 pm				
3:30 pm				
4:00 pm				
4:30 pm				
5:00 pm				
5:30 pm				
6:00 pm				
6:30 pm				
7:00 pm				
7:30 pm				
8:00 pm				
8:30 pm				

	SUNDAY	MONDAY	TUESDAY	WEDNESDAY

July - Aug LESSON PLANS Week of 28th - 3rd

THURSDAY	FRIDAY	SATURDAY

Weekly Supplies

☐ _____
☐ _____
☐ _____
☐ _____
☐ _____
☐ _____
☐ _____
☐ _____
☐ _____
☐ _____
☐ _____
☐ _____

To Dos

☐ _____
☐ _____
☐ _____
☐ _____
☐ _____
☐ _____
☐ _____
☐ _____
☐ _____
☐ _____
☐ _____

Notes

☐ _____
☐ _____
☐ _____
☐ _____
☐ _____
☐ _____
☐ _____
☐ _____
☐ _____

Weekly Schedule

	SUNDAY	MONDAY	TUESDAY
7:00 am			
7:30 am			
8:00 am			
8:30 am			
9:00 am			
9:30 am			
10:00 am			
10:30 am			
11:00 am			
11:30 am			
12:00 pm			
12:30 pm			
1:00 pm			
1:30 pm			
2:00 pm			
2:30 pm			
3:00 pm			
3:30 pm			
4:00 pm			
4:30 pm			
5:00 pm			
5:30 pm			
6:00 pm			
6:30 pm			
7:00 pm			
7:30 pm			
8:00 pm			
8:30 pm			

July-Aug

Week of 28th - 3rd

	WEDNESDAY	THURSDAY	FRIDAY	SATURDAY
7:00 am				
7:30 am				
8:00 am				
8:30 am				
9:00 am				
9:30 am				
10:00 am				
10:30 am				
11:00 am				
11:30 am				
12:00 pm				
12:30 pm				
1:00 pm				
1:30 pm				
2:00 pm				
2:30 pm				
3:00 pm				
3:30 pm				
4:00 pm				
4:30 pm				
5:00 pm				
5:30 pm				
6:00 pm				
6:30 pm				
7:00 pm				
7:30 pm				
8:00 pm				
8:30 pm				

August 2024

SUNDAY	MONDAY	TUESDAY	WEDNESDAY
4	5	6	7
11	12	13	14
18	19	20	21
25	26	27	28

THURSDAY	FRIDAY	SATURDAY	NOTES
1	2	3	
8	9	10	
15	16	17	
22	23	24	
29	30	31	

	SUNDAY	MONDAY	TUESDAY	WEDNESDAY

August LESSON PLANS Week of 4th - 10th

THURSDAY	FRIDAY	SATURDAY

Weekly Supplies

- [ ]
- [ ]
- [ ]
- [ ]
- [ ]
- [ ]
- [ ]
- [ ]
- [ ]
- [ ]
- [ ]
- [ ]

To Dos

- [ ]
- [ ]
- [ ]
- [ ]
- [ ]
- [ ]
- [ ]
- [ ]
- [ ]
- [ ]
- [ ]
- [ ]

Notes

- [ ]
- [ ]
- [ ]
- [ ]
- [ ]
- [ ]
- [ ]
- [ ]
- [ ]

Weekly Schedule

	SUNDAY	MONDAY	TUESDAY
7:00 am			
7:30 am			
8:00 am			
8:30 am			
9:00 am			
9:30 am			
10:00 am			
10:30 am			
11:00 am			
11:30 am			
12:00 pm			
12:30 pm			
1:00 pm			
1:30 pm			
2:00 pm			
2:30 pm			
3:00 pm			
3:30 pm			
4:00 pm			
4:30 pm			
5:00 pm			
5:30 pm			
6:00 pm			
6:30 pm			
7:00 pm			
7:30 pm			
8:00 pm			
8:30 pm			

August

Week of 4th - 10th

	WEDNESDAY	THURSDAY	FRIDAY	SATURDAY
7:00 am				
7:30 am				
8:00 am				
8:30 am				
9:00 am				
9:30 am				
10:00 am				
10:30 am				
11:00 am				
11:30 am				
12:00 pm				
12:30 pm				
1:00 pm				
1:30 pm				
2:00 pm				
2:30 pm				
3:00 pm				
3:30 pm				
4:00 pm				
4:30 pm				
5:00 pm				
5:30 pm				
6:00 pm				
6:30 pm				
7:00 pm				
7:30 pm				
8:00 pm				
8:30 pm				

	SUNDAY	MONDAY	TUESDAY	WEDNESDAY
	SUNDAY	MONDAY	TUESDAY	WEDNESDAY

August LESSON PLANS   Week of 11th – 17th

THURSDAY	FRIDAY	SATURDAY

Weekly Supplies

- [ ] _____
- [ ] _____
- [ ] _____
- [ ] _____
- [ ] _____
- [ ] _____
- [ ] _____
- [ ] _____
- [ ] _____
- [ ] _____
- [ ] _____
- [ ] _____

To Dos

- [ ] _____
- [ ] _____
- [ ] _____
- [ ] _____
- [ ] _____
- [ ] _____
- [ ] _____
- [ ] _____
- [ ] _____
- [ ] _____
- [ ] _____

Notes

- [ ] _____
- [ ] _____
- [ ] _____
- [ ] _____
- [ ] _____
- [ ] _____
- [ ] _____
- [ ] _____
- [ ] _____

Weekly Schedule

	SUNDAY	MONDAY	TUESDAY
7:00 am			
7:30 am			
8:00 am			
8:30 am			
9:00 am			
9:30 am			
10:00 am			
10:30 am			
11:00 am			
11:30 am			
12:00 pm			
12:30 pm			
1:00 pm			
1:30 pm			
2:00 pm			
2:30 pm			
3:00 pm			
3:30 pm			
4:00 pm			
4:30 pm			
5:00 pm			
5:30 pm			
6:00 pm			
6:30 pm			
7:00 pm			
7:30 pm			
8:00 pm			
8:30 pm			

August

Week of 11th - 17th

	WEDNESDAY	THURSDAY	FRIDAY	SATURDAY
7:00 am				
7:30 am				
8:00 am				
8:30 am				
9:00 am				
9:30 am				
10:00 am				
10:30 am				
11:00 am				
11:30 am				
12:00 pm				
12:30 pm				
1:00 pm				
1:30 pm				
2:00 pm				
2:30 pm				
3:00 pm				
3:30 pm				
4:00 pm				
4:30 pm				
5:00 pm				
5:30 pm				
6:00 pm				
6:30 pm				
7:00 pm				
7:30 pm				
8:00 pm				
8:30 pm				

August LESSON PLANS Week of 18th - 24th

	SUNDAY	MONDAY	TUESDAY	WEDNESDAY

THURSDAY	FRIDAY	SATURDAY

Weekly Supplies

- [ ] _____
- [ ] _____
- [ ] _____
- [ ] _____
- [ ] _____
- [ ] _____
- [ ] _____
- [ ] _____
- [ ] _____
- [ ] _____
- [ ] _____
- [ ] _____

To Dos

- [ ] _____
- [ ] _____
- [ ] _____
- [ ] _____
- [ ] _____
- [ ] _____
- [ ] _____
- [ ] _____
- [ ] _____
- [ ] _____
- [ ] _____

Notes

- [ ] _____
- [ ] _____
- [ ] _____
- [ ] _____
- [ ] _____
- [ ] _____
- [ ] _____
- [ ] _____
- [ ] _____

Weekly Schedule

	SUNDAY	MONDAY	TUESDAY
7:00 am			
7:30 am			
8:00 am			
8:30 am			
9:00 am			
9:30 am			
10:00 am			
10:30 am			
11:00 am			
11:30 am			
12:00 pm			
12:30 pm			
1:00 pm			
1:30 pm			
2:00 pm			
2:30 pm			
3:00 pm			
3:30 pm			
4:00 pm			
4:30 pm			
5:00 pm			
5:30 pm			
6:00 pm			
6:30 pm			
7:00 pm			
7:30 pm			
8:00 pm			
8:30 pm			

August

Week of 18th - 24th

	WEDNESDAY	THURSDAY	FRIDAY	SATURDAY
7:00 am				
7:30 am				
8:00 am				
8:30 am				
9:00 am				
9:30 am				
10:00 am				
10:30 am				
11:00 am				
11:30 am				
12:00 pm				
12:30 pm				
1:00 pm				
1:30 pm				
2:00 pm				
2:30 pm				
3:00 pm				
3:30 pm				
4:00 pm				
4:30 pm				
5:00 pm				
5:30 pm				
6:00 pm				
6:30 pm				
7:00 pm				
7:30 pm				
8:00 pm				
8:30 pm				

August LESSON PLANS   Week of 25th – 31st

	SUNDAY	MONDAY	TUESDAY	WEDNESDAY

THURSDAY	FRIDAY	SATURDAY

Weekly Supplies

☐ _____
☐ _____
☐ _____
☐ _____
☐ _____
☐ _____
☐ _____
☐ _____
☐ _____
☐ _____
☐ _____
☐ _____

To Dos

☐ _____
☐ _____
☐ _____
☐ _____
☐ _____
☐ _____
☐ _____
☐ _____
☐ _____
☐ _____
☐ _____
☐ _____

Notes

☐ _____
☐ _____
☐ _____
☐ _____
☐ _____
☐ _____
☐ _____
☐ _____
☐ _____

Weekly Schedule

	SUNDAY	MONDAY	TUESDAY
7:00 am			
7:30 am			
8:00 am			
8:30 am			
9:00 am			
9:30 am			
10:00 am			
10:30 am			
11:00 am			
11:30 am			
12:00 pm			
12:30 pm			
1:00 pm			
1:30 pm			
2:00 pm			
2:30 pm			
3:00 pm			
3:30 pm			
4:00 pm			
4:30 pm			
5:00 pm			
5:30 pm			
6:00 pm			
6:30 pm			
7:00 pm			
7:30 pm			
8:00 pm			
8:30 pm			

August

Week of 25th - 31st

	WEDNESDAY	THURSDAY	FRIDAY	SATURDAY
7:00 am				
7:30 am				
8:00 am				
8:30 am				
9:00 am				
9:30 am				
10:00 am				
10:30 am				
11:00 am				
11:30 am				
12:00 pm				
12:30 pm				
1:00 pm				
1:30 pm				
2:00 pm				
2:30 pm				
3:00 pm				
3:30 pm				
4:00 pm				
4:30 pm				
5:00 pm				
5:30 pm				
6:00 pm				
6:30 pm				
7:00 pm				
7:30 pm				
8:00 pm				
8:30 pm				

September 2024

SUNDAY	MONDAY	TUESDAY	WEDNESDAY
1	2	3	4
8	9	10	11
15	16	17	18
22	23	24	25
29	30		

THURSDAY	FRIDAY	SATURDAY	NOTES
5	6	7	
12	13	14	
19	20	21	
26	27	28	

	SUNDAY	MONDAY	TUESDAY	WEDNESDAY

September LESSON PLANS Week of 1st - 7th

THURSDAY	FRIDAY	SATURDAY

☐ _____
☐ _____
☐ _____
☐ _____
☐ _____
☐ _____
☐ _____
☐ _____
☐ _____
☐ _____
☐ _____
☐ _____

To Dos

☐ _____
☐ _____
☐ _____
☐ _____
☐ _____
☐ _____
☐ _____
☐ _____
☐ _____
☐ _____
☐ _____
☐ _____

Notes

☐ _____
☐ _____
☐ _____
☐ _____
☐ _____
☐ _____
☐ _____
☐ _____
☐ _____

Weekly Schedule

	SUNDAY	MONDAY	TUESDAY
7:00 am			
7:30 am			
8:00 am			
8:30 am			
9:00 am			
9:30 am			
10:00 am			
10:30 am			
11:00 am			
11:30 am			
12:00 pm			
12:30 pm			
1:00 pm			
1:30 pm			
2:00 pm			
2:30 pm			
3:00 pm			
3:30 pm			
4:00 pm			
4:30 pm			
5:00 pm			
5:30 pm			
6:00 pm			
6:30 pm			
7:00 pm			
7:30 pm			
8:00 pm			
8:30 pm			

September Week of 1st - 7th

	WEDNESDAY	THURSDAY	FRIDAY	SATURDAY
7:00 am				
7:30 am				
8:00 am				
8:30 am				
9:00 am				
9:30 am				
10:00 am				
10:30 am				
11:00 am				
11:30 am				
12:00 pm				
12:30 pm				
1:00 pm				
1:30 pm				
2:00 pm				
2:30 pm				
3:00 pm				
3:30 pm				
4:00 pm				
4:30 pm				
5:00 pm				
5:30 pm				
6:00 pm				
6:30 pm				
7:00 pm				
7:30 pm				
8:00 pm				
8:30 pm				

	SUNDAY	MONDAY	TUESDAY	WEDNESDAY

September LESSON PLANS Week of 8th – 14th

THURSDAY	FRIDAY	SATURDAY

Weekly Supplies

- [ ] _____
- [ ] _____
- [ ] _____
- [ ] _____
- [ ] _____
- [ ] _____
- [ ] _____
- [ ] _____
- [ ] _____
- [ ] _____
- [ ] _____
- [ ] _____

To Dos

- [ ] _____
- [ ] _____
- [ ] _____
- [ ] _____
- [ ] _____
- [ ] _____
- [ ] _____
- [ ] _____
- [ ] _____
- [ ] _____
- [ ] _____

Notes

- [ ] _____
- [ ] _____
- [ ] _____
- [ ] _____
- [ ] _____
- [ ] _____
- [ ] _____
- [ ] _____
- [ ] _____

Weekly Schedule

	SUNDAY	MONDAY	TUESDAY
7:00 am			
7:30 am			
8:00 am			
8:30 am			
9:00 am			
9:30 am			
10:00 am			
10:30 am			
11:00 am			
11:30 am			
12:00 pm			
12:30 pm			
1:00 pm			
1:30 pm			
2:00 pm			
2:30 pm			
3:00 pm			
3:30 pm			
4:00 pm			
4:30 pm			
5:00 pm			
5:30 pm			
6:00 pm			
6:30 pm			
7:00 pm			
7:30 pm			
8:00 pm			
8:30 pm			

September

Week of 8th - 14th

	WEDNESDAY	THURSDAY	FRIDAY	SATURDAY
7:00 am				
7:30 am				
8:00 am				
8:30 am				
9:00 am				
9:30 am				
10:00 am				
10:30 am				
11:00 am				
11:30 am				
12:00 pm				
12:30 pm				
1:00 pm				
1:30 pm				
2:00 pm				
2:30 pm				
3:00 pm				
3:30 pm				
4:00 pm				
4:30 pm				
5:00 pm				
5:30 pm				
6:00 pm				
6:30 pm				
7:00 pm				
7:30 pm				
8:00 pm				
8:30 pm				

	SUNDAY	MONDAY	TUESDAY	WEDNESDAY

September LESSON PLANS Week of 15th - 21st

THURSDAY	FRIDAY	SATURDAY

Weekly Supplies

☐ _____
☐ _____
☐ _____
☐ _____
☐ _____
☐ _____
☐ _____
☐ _____
☐ _____
☐ _____
☐ _____
☐ _____

To Dos

☐ _____
☐ _____
☐ _____
☐ _____
☐ _____
☐ _____
☐ _____
☐ _____
☐ _____
☐ _____
☐ _____

Notes

☐ _____
☐ _____
☐ _____
☐ _____
☐ _____
☐ _____
☐ _____
☐ _____
☐ _____

Weekly Schedule

	SUNDAY	MONDAY	TUESDAY
7:00 am			
7:30 am			
8:00 am			
8:30 am			
9:00 am			
9:30 am			
10:00 am			
10:30 am			
11:00 am			
11:30 am			
12:00 pm			
12:30 pm			
1:00 pm			
1:30 pm			
2:00 pm			
2:30 pm			
3:00 pm			
3:30 pm			
4:00 pm			
4:30 pm			
5:00 pm			
5:30 pm			
6:00 pm			
6:30 pm			
7:00 pm			
7:30 pm			
8:00 pm			
8:30 pm			

September

Week of 15th - 21st

	WEDNESDAY	THURSDAY	FRIDAY	SATURDAY
7:00 am				
7:30 am				
8:00 am				
8:30 am				
9:00 am				
9:30 am				
10:00 am				
10:30 am				
11:00 am				
11:30 am				
12:00 pm				
12:30 pm				
1:00 pm				
1:30 pm				
2:00 pm				
2:30 pm				
3:00 pm				
3:30 pm				
4:00 pm				
4:30 pm				
5:00 pm				
5:30 pm				
6:00 pm				
6:30 pm				
7:00 pm				
7:30 pm				
8:00 pm				
8:30 pm				

September LESSON PLANS Week of 22nd- 28th

	SUNDAY	MONDAY	TUESDAY	WEDNESDAY

THURSDAY	FRIDAY	SATURDAY

Weekly Supplies

☐ _____
☐ _____
☐ _____
☐ _____
☐ _____
☐ _____
☐ _____
☐ _____
☐ _____
☐ _____
☐ _____
☐ _____

To Dos

☐ _____
☐ _____
☐ _____
☐ _____
☐ _____
☐ _____
☐ _____
☐ _____
☐ _____
☐ _____
☐ _____
☐ _____

Notes

☐ _____
☐ _____
☐ _____
☐ _____
☐ _____
☐ _____
☐ _____
☐ _____
☐ _____

Weekly Schedule

	SUNDAY	MONDAY	TUESDAY
7:00 am			
7:30 am			
8:00 am			
8:30 am			
9:00 am			
9:30 am			
10:00 am			
10:30 am			
11:00 am			
11:30 am			
12:00 pm			
12:30 pm			
1:00 pm			
1:30 pm			
2:00 pm			
2:30 pm			
3:00 pm			
3:30 pm			
4:00 pm			
4:30 pm			
5:00 pm			
5:30 pm			
6:00 pm			
6:30 pm			
7:00 pm			
7:30 pm			
8:00 pm			
8:30 pm			

September
Week of 22nd - 28th

	WEDNESDAY	THURSDAY	FRIDAY	SATURDAY
7:00 am				
7:30 am				
8:00 am				
8:30 am				
9:00 am				
9:30 am				
10:00 am				
10:30 am				
11:00 am				
11:30 am				
12:00 pm				
12:30 pm				
1:00 pm				
1:30 pm				
2:00 pm				
2:30 pm				
3:00 pm				
3:30 pm				
4:00 pm				
4:30 pm				
5:00 pm				
5:30 pm				
6:00 pm				
6:30 pm				
7:00 pm				
7:30 pm				
8:00 pm				
8:30 pm				

October 2024

SUNDAY	MONDAY	TUESDAY	WEDNESDAY
		1	2
6	7	8	9
13	14	15	16
20	21	22	23
27	28	29	30

THURSDAY	FRIDAY	SATURDAY	NOTES
3	4	5	
10	11	12	
17	18	19	
24	25	26	
31			

	SUNDAY	MONDAY	TUESDAY	WEDNESDAY

Sept-Oct LESSON PLANS Week of 29th- 5th

THURSDAY	FRIDAY	SATURDAY

Weekly Supplies

☐ _____
☐ _____
☐ _____
☐ _____
☐ _____
☐ _____
☐ _____
☐ _____
☐ _____
☐ _____
☐ _____
☐ _____

To Dos

☐ _____
☐ _____
☐ _____
☐ _____
☐ _____
☐ _____
☐ _____
☐ _____
☐ _____
☐ _____
☐ _____

Notes

☐ _____
☐ _____
☐ _____
☐ _____
☐ _____
☐ _____
☐ _____
☐ _____
☐ _____

Weekly Schedule

	SUNDAY	MONDAY	TUESDAY
7:00 am			
7:30 am			
8:00 am			
8:30 am			
9:00 am			
9:30 am			
10:00 am			
10:30 am			
11:00 am			
11:30 am			
12:00 pm			
12:30 pm			
1:00 pm			
1:30 pm			
2:00 pm			
2:30 pm			
3:00 pm			
3:30 pm			
4:00 pm			
4:30 pm			
5:00 pm			
5:30 pm			
6:00 pm			
6:30 pm			
7:00 pm			
7:30 pm			
8:00 pm			
8:30 pm			

Sept-Oct

Week of 29th - 5th

	WEDNESDAY	THURSDAY	FRIDAY	SATURDAY
7:00 am				
7:30 am				
8:00 am				
8:30 am				
9:00 am				
9:30 am				
10:00 am				
10:30 am				
11:00 am				
11:30 am				
12:00 pm				
12:30 pm				
1:00 pm				
1:30 pm				
2:00 pm				
2:30 pm				
3:00 pm				
3:30 pm				
4:00 pm				
4:30 pm				
5:00 pm				
5:30 pm				
6:00 pm				
6:30 pm				
7:00 pm				
7:30 pm				
8:00 pm				
8:30 pm				

	SUNDAY	MONDAY	TUESDAY	WEDNESDAY

October LESSON PLANS Week of 6th - 12th

	SUNDAY	MONDAY	TUESDAY	WEDNESDAY

THURSDAY	FRIDAY	SATURDAY

Weekly Supplies

- [ ] _____
- [ ] _____
- [ ] _____
- [ ] _____
- [ ] _____
- [ ] _____
- [ ] _____
- [ ] _____
- [ ] _____
- [ ] _____
- [ ] _____
- [ ] _____

To Dos

- [ ] _____
- [ ] _____
- [ ] _____
- [ ] _____
- [ ] _____
- [ ] _____
- [ ] _____
- [ ] _____
- [ ] _____
- [ ] _____
- [ ] _____

Notes

- [ ] _____
- [ ] _____
- [ ] _____
- [ ] _____
- [ ] _____
- [ ] _____
- [ ] _____
- [ ] _____
- [ ] _____

Weekly Schedule

	SUNDAY	MONDAY	TUESDAY
7:00 am			
7:30 am			
8:00 am			
8:30 am			
9:00 am			
9:30 am			
10:00 am			
10:30 am			
11:00 am			
11:30 am			
12:00 pm			
12:30 pm			
1:00 pm			
1:30 pm			
2:00 pm			
2:30 pm			
3:00 pm			
3:30 pm			
4:00 pm			
4:30 pm			
5:00 pm			
5:30 pm			
6:00 pm			
6:30 pm			
7:00 pm			
7:30 pm			
8:00 pm			
8:30 pm			

October

Week of 6th - 12th

	WEDNESDAY	THURSDAY	FRIDAY	SATURDAY
7:00 am				
7:30 am				
8:00 am				
8:30 am				
9:00 am				
9:30 am				
10:00 am				
10:30 am				
11:00 am				
11:30 am				
12:00 pm				
12:30 pm				
1:00 pm				
1:30 pm				
2:00 pm				
2:30 pm				
3:00 pm				
3:30 pm				
4:00 pm				
4:30 pm				
5:00 pm				
5:30 pm				
6:00 pm				
6:30 pm				
7:00 pm				
7:30 pm				
8:00 pm				
8:30 pm				

October LESSON PLANS Week of 13th - 19th

	SUNDAY	MONDAY	TUESDAY	WEDNESDAY

THURSDAY	FRIDAY	SATURDAY

Weekly Supplies

☐ _____
☐ _____
☐ _____
☐ _____
☐ _____
☐ _____
☐ _____
☐ _____
☐ _____
☐ _____
☐ _____
☐ _____

To Dos

☐ _____
☐ _____
☐ _____
☐ _____
☐ _____
☐ _____
☐ _____
☐ _____
☐ _____
☐ _____
☐ _____

Notes

☐ _____
☐ _____
☐ _____
☐ _____
☐ _____
☐ _____
☐ _____
☐ _____
☐ _____

Weekly Schedule

	SUNDAY	MONDAY	TUESDAY
7:00 am			
7:30 am			
8:00 am			
8:30 am			
9:00 am			
9:30 am			
10:00 am			
10:30 am			
11:00 am			
11:30 am			
12:00 pm			
12:30 pm			
1:00 pm			
1:30 pm			
2:00 pm			
2:30 pm			
3:00 pm			
3:30 pm			
4:00 pm			
4:30 pm			
5:00 pm			
5:30 pm			
6:00 pm			
6:30 pm			
7:00 pm			
7:30 pm			
8:00 pm			
8:30 pm			

October

Week of 13th - 19th

	WEDNESDAY	THURSDAY	FRIDAY	SATURDAY
7:00 am				
7:30 am				
8:00 am				
8:30 am				
9:00 am				
9:30 am				
10:00 am				
10:30 am				
11:00 am				
11:30 am				
12:00 pm				
12:30 pm				
1:00 pm				
1:30 pm				
2:00 pm				
2:30 pm				
3:00 pm				
3:30 pm				
4:00 pm				
4:30 pm				
5:00 pm				
5:30 pm				
6:00 pm				
6:30 pm				
7:00 pm				
7:30 pm				
8:00 pm				
8:30 pm				

	SUNDAY	MONDAY	TUESDAY	WEDNESDAY

October LESSON PLANS Week of 20th - 26th

THURSDAY	FRIDAY	SATURDAY

Weekly Supplies

- [ ] _____
- [ ] _____
- [ ] _____
- [ ] _____
- [ ] _____
- [ ] _____
- [ ] _____
- [ ] _____
- [ ] _____
- [ ] _____
- [ ] _____
- [ ] _____

To Dos

- [ ] _____
- [ ] _____
- [ ] _____
- [ ] _____
- [ ] _____
- [ ] _____
- [ ] _____
- [ ] _____
- [ ] _____
- [ ] _____
- [ ] _____

Notes

- [ ] _____
- [ ] _____
- [ ] _____
- [ ] _____
- [ ] _____
- [ ] _____
- [ ] _____
- [ ] _____
- [ ] _____

Weekly Schedule

	SUNDAY	MONDAY	TUESDAY
7:00 am			
7:30 am			
8:00 am			
8:30 am			
9:00 am			
9:30 am			
10:00 am			
10:30 am			
11:00 am			
11:30 am			
12:00 pm			
12:30 pm			
1:00 pm			
1:30 pm			
2:00 pm			
2:30 pm			
3:00 pm			
3:30 pm			
4:00 pm			
4:30 pm			
5:00 pm			
5:30 pm			
6:00 pm			
6:30 pm			
7:00 pm			
7:30 pm			
8:00 pm			
8:30 pm			

October

Week of 20th - 26th

	WEDNESDAY	THURSDAY	FRIDAY	SATURDAY
7:00 am				
7:30 am				
8:00 am				
8:30 am				
9:00 am				
9:30 am				
10:00 am				
10:30 am				
11:00 am				
11:30 am				
12:00 pm				
12:30 pm				
1:00 pm				
1:30 pm				
2:00 pm				
2:30 pm				
3:00 pm				
3:30 pm				
4:00 pm				
4:30 pm				
5:00 pm				
5:30 pm				
6:00 pm				
6:30 pm				
7:00 pm				
7:30 pm				
8:00 pm				
8:30 pm				

Oct-Nov LESSON PLANS Week of 27th - 2nd

	SUNDAY	MONDAY	TUESDAY	WEDNESDAY

THURSDAY	FRIDAY	SATURDAY

Weekly Supplies

- ☐ _____
- ☐ _____
- ☐ _____
- ☐ _____
- ☐ _____
- ☐ _____
- ☐ _____
- ☐ _____
- ☐ _____
- ☐ _____
- ☐ _____
- ☐ _____

To Dos

- ☐ _____
- ☐ _____
- ☐ _____
- ☐ _____
- ☐ _____
- ☐ _____
- ☐ _____
- ☐ _____
- ☐ _____
- ☐ _____
- ☐ _____

Notes

- ☐ _____
- ☐ _____
- ☐ _____
- ☐ _____
- ☐ _____
- ☐ _____
- ☐ _____
- ☐ _____
- ☐ _____

Weekly Schedule

	SUNDAY	MONDAY	TUESDAY
7:00 am			
7:30 am			
8:00 am			
8:30 am			
9:00 am			
9:30 am			
10:00 am			
10:30 am			
11:00 am			
11:30 am			
12:00 pm			
12:30 pm			
1:00 pm			
1:30 pm			
2:00 pm			
2:30 pm			
3:00 pm			
3:30 pm			
4:00 pm			
4:30 pm			
5:00 pm			
5:30 pm			
6:00 pm			
6:30 pm			
7:00 pm			
7:30 pm			
8:00 pm			
8:30 pm			

Oct-Nov

Week of 27th - 2nd

	WEDNESDAY	THURSDAY	FRIDAY	SATURDAY
7:00 am				
7:30 am				
8:00 am				
8:30 am				
9:00 am				
9:30 am				
10:00 am				
10:30 am				
11:00 am				
11:30 am				
12:00 pm				
12:30 pm				
1:00 pm				
1:30 pm				
2:00 pm				
2:30 pm				
3:00 pm				
3:30 pm				
4:00 pm				
4:30 pm				
5:00 pm				
5:30 pm				
6:00 pm				
6:30 pm				
7:00 pm				
7:30 pm				
8:00 pm				
8:30 pm				

November 2024

SUNDAY	MONDAY	TUESDAY	WEDNESDAY
3	4	5	6
10	11	12	13
17	18	19	20
24	25	26	27

THURSDAY	FRIDAY	SATURDAY	NOTES
	1	2	
7	8	9	
14	15	16	
21	22	23	
28	29	30	

November

LESSON PLANS — Week of 3rd - 9th

	SUNDAY	MONDAY	TUESDAY	WEDNESDAY
	SUNDAY	MONDAY	TUESDAY	WEDNESDAY

THURSDAY	FRIDAY	SATURDAY

Weekly Supplies

- ☐ _____
- ☐ _____
- ☐ _____
- ☐ _____
- ☐ _____
- ☐ _____
- ☐ _____
- ☐ _____
- ☐ _____
- ☐ _____
- ☐ _____
- ☐ _____

To Dos

- ☐ _____
- ☐ _____
- ☐ _____
- ☐ _____
- ☐ _____
- ☐ _____
- ☐ _____
- ☐ _____
- ☐ _____
- ☐ _____
- ☐ _____

Notes

- ☐ _____
- ☐ _____
- ☐ _____
- ☐ _____
- ☐ _____
- ☐ _____
- ☐ _____
- ☐ _____
- ☐ _____

Weekly Schedule

	SUNDAY	MONDAY	TUESDAY
7:00 am			
7:30 am			
8:00 am			
8:30 am			
9:00 am			
9:30 am			
10:00 am			
10:30 am			
11:00 am			
11:30 am			
12:00 pm			
12:30 pm			
1:00 pm			
1:30 pm			
2:00 pm			
2:30 pm			
3:00 pm			
3:30 pm			
4:00 pm			
4:30 pm			
5:00 pm			
5:30 pm			
6:00 pm			
6:30 pm			
7:00 pm			
7:30 pm			
8:00 pm			
8:30 pm			

November

Week of 3rd - 9th

	WEDNESDAY	THURSDAY	FRIDAY	SATURDAY
7:00 am				
7:30 am				
8:00 am				
8:30 am				
9:00 am				
9:30 am				
10:00 am				
10:30 am				
11:00 am				
11:30 am				
12:00 pm				
12:30 pm				
1:00 pm				
1:30 pm				
2:00 pm				
2:30 pm				
3:00 pm				
3:30 pm				
4:00 pm				
4:30 pm				
5:00 pm				
5:30 pm				
6:00 pm				
6:30 pm				
7:00 pm				
7:30 pm				
8:00 pm				
8:30 pm				

November LESSON PLANS   Week of 10th - 16th

	SUNDAY	MONDAY	TUESDAY	WEDNESDAY

THURSDAY	FRIDAY	SATURDAY

Weekly Supplies

☐ _____
☐ _____
☐ _____
☐ _____
☐ _____
☐ _____
☐ _____
☐ _____
☐ _____
☐ _____
☐ _____
☐ _____

To Dos

☐ _____
☐ _____
☐ _____
☐ _____
☐ _____
☐ _____
☐ _____
☐ _____
☐ _____
☐ _____
☐ _____

Notes

☐ _____
☐ _____
☐ _____
☐ _____
☐ _____
☐ _____
☐ _____
☐ _____
☐ _____

Weekly Schedule

	SUNDAY	MONDAY	TUESDAY
7:00 am			
7:30 am			
8:00 am			
8:30 am			
9:00 am			
9:30 am			
10:00 am			
10:30 am			
11:00 am			
11:30 am			
12:00 pm			
12:30 pm			
1:00 pm			
1:30 pm			
2:00 pm			
2:30 pm			
3:00 pm			
3:30 pm			
4:00 pm			
4:30 pm			
5:00 pm			
5:30 pm			
6:00 pm			
6:30 pm			
7:00 pm			
7:30 pm			
8:00 pm			
8:30 pm			

November
Week of 10th - 16th

	WEDNESDAY	THURSDAY	FRIDAY	SATURDAY
7:00 am				
7:30 am				
8:00 am				
8:30 am				
9:00 am				
9:30 am				
10:00 am				
10:30 am				
11:00 am				
11:30 am				
12:00 pm				
12:30 pm				
1:00 pm				
1:30 pm				
2:00 pm				
2:30 pm				
3:00 pm				
3:30 pm				
4:00 pm				
4:30 pm				
5:00 pm				
5:30 pm				
6:00 pm				
6:30 pm				
7:00 pm				
7:30 pm				
8:00 pm				
8:30 pm				

November LESSON PLANS   Week of 17th - 23rd

	SUNDAY	MONDAY	TUESDAY	WEDNESDAY

THURSDAY	FRIDAY	SATURDAY

Weekly Supplies

- [ ] _____
- [ ] _____
- [ ] _____
- [ ] _____
- [ ] _____
- [ ] _____
- [ ] _____
- [ ] _____
- [ ] _____
- [ ] _____
- [ ] _____
- [ ] _____

To Dos

- [ ] _____
- [ ] _____
- [ ] _____
- [ ] _____
- [ ] _____
- [ ] _____
- [ ] _____
- [ ] _____
- [ ] _____
- [ ] _____
- [ ] _____

Notes

- [ ] _____
- [ ] _____
- [ ] _____
- [ ] _____
- [ ] _____
- [ ] _____
- [ ] _____
- [ ] _____
- [ ] _____

Weekly Schedule

	SUNDAY	MONDAY	TUESDAY
7:00 am			
7:30 am			
8:00 am			
8:30 am			
9:00 am			
9:30 am			
10:00 am			
10:30 am			
11:00 am			
11:30 am			
12:00 pm			
12:30 pm			
1:00 pm			
1:30 pm			
2:00 pm			
2:30 pm			
3:00 pm			
3:30 pm			
4:00 pm			
4:30 pm			
5:00 pm			
5:30 pm			
6:00 pm			
6:30 pm			
7:00 pm			
7:30 pm			
8:00 pm			
8:30 pm			

November

Week of 17th - 23rd

	WEDNESDAY	THURSDAY	FRIDAY	SATURDAY
7:00 am				
7:30 am				
8:00 am				
8:30 am				
9:00 am				
9:30 am				
10:00 am				
10:30 am				
11:00 am				
11:30 am				
12:00 pm				
12:30 pm				
1:00 pm				
1:30 pm				
2:00 pm				
2:30 pm				
3:00 pm				
3:30 pm				
4:00 pm				
4:30 pm				
5:00 pm				
5:30 pm				
6:00 pm				
6:30 pm				
7:00 pm				
7:30 pm				
8:00 pm				
8:30 pm				

November LESSON PLANS Week of 24th - 30th

	SUNDAY	MONDAY	TUESDAY	WEDNESDAY

THURSDAY	FRIDAY	SATURDAY

Weekly Supplies

- [ ] _____
- [ ] _____
- [ ] _____
- [ ] _____
- [ ] _____
- [ ] _____
- [ ] _____
- [ ] _____
- [ ] _____
- [ ] _____
- [ ] _____
- [ ] _____

To Dos

- [ ] _____
- [ ] _____
- [ ] _____
- [ ] _____
- [ ] _____
- [ ] _____
- [ ] _____
- [ ] _____
- [ ] _____
- [ ] _____
- [ ] _____

Notes

- [ ] _____
- [ ] _____
- [ ] _____
- [ ] _____
- [ ] _____
- [ ] _____
- [ ] _____
- [ ] _____
- [ ] _____

Weekly Schedule

	SUNDAY	MONDAY	TUESDAY
7:00 am			
7:30 am			
8:00 am			
8:30 am			
9:00 am			
9:30 am			
10:00 am			
10:30 am			
11:00 am			
11:30 am			
12:00 pm			
12:30 pm			
1:00 pm			
1:30 pm			
2:00 pm			
2:30 pm			
3:00 pm			
3:30 pm			
4:00 pm			
4:30 pm			
5:00 pm			
5:30 pm			
6:00 pm			
6:30 pm			
7:00 pm			
7:30 pm			
8:00 pm			
8:30 pm			

November

Week of 24th - 30th

	WEDNESDAY	THURSDAY	FRIDAY	SATURDAY
7:00 am				
7:30 am				
8:00 am				
8:30 am				
9:00 am				
9:30 am				
10:00 am				
10:30 am				
11:00 am				
11:30 am				
12:00 pm				
12:30 pm				
1:00 pm				
1:30 pm				
2:00 pm				
2:30 pm				
3:00 pm				
3:30 pm				
4:00 pm				
4:30 pm				
5:00 pm				
5:30 pm				
6:00 pm				
6:30 pm				
7:00 pm				
7:30 pm				
8:00 pm				
8:30 pm				

December 2024

SUNDAY	MONDAY	TUESDAY	WEDNESDAY
1	2	3	4
8	9	10	11
15	16	17	18
22	23	24	25
29	30	31	

THURSDAY	FRIDAY	SATURDAY	NOTES
5	6	7	
12	13	14	
19	20	21	
26	27	28	

	SUNDAY	MONDAY	TUESDAY	WEDNESDAY

December LESSON PLANS Week of 1st - 7th

THURSDAY	FRIDAY	SATURDAY

Weekly Supplies

- [ ] _____
- [ ] _____
- [ ] _____
- [ ] _____
- [ ] _____
- [ ] _____
- [ ] _____
- [ ] _____
- [ ] _____
- [ ] _____
- [ ] _____
- [ ] _____

To Dos

- [ ] _____
- [ ] _____
- [ ] _____
- [ ] _____
- [ ] _____
- [ ] _____
- [ ] _____
- [ ] _____
- [ ] _____
- [ ] _____
- [ ] _____
- [ ] _____

Notes

- [ ] _____
- [ ] _____
- [ ] _____
- [ ] _____
- [ ] _____
- [ ] _____
- [ ] _____
- [ ] _____
- [ ] _____

Weekly Schedule

	SUNDAY	MONDAY	TUESDAY
7:00 am			
7:30 am			
8:00 am			
8:30 am			
9:00 am			
9:30 am			
10:00 am			
10:30 am			
11:00 am			
11:30 am			
12:00 pm			
12:30 pm			
1:00 pm			
1:30 pm			
2:00 pm			
2:30 pm			
3:00 pm			
3:30 pm			
4:00 pm			
4:30 pm			
5:00 pm			
5:30 pm			
6:00 pm			
6:30 pm			
7:00 pm			
7:30 pm			
8:00 pm			
8:30 pm			

December

Week of 1st - 7th

	WEDNESDAY	THURSDAY	FRIDAY	SATURDAY
7:00 am				
7:30 am				
8:00 am				
8:30 am				
9:00 am				
9:30 am				
10:00 am				
10:30 am				
11:00 am				
11:30 am				
12:00 pm				
12:30 pm				
1:00 pm				
1:30 pm				
2:00 pm				
2:30 pm				
3:00 pm				
3:30 pm				
4:00 pm				
4:30 pm				
5:00 pm				
5:30 pm				
6:00 pm				
6:30 pm				
7:00 pm				
7:30 pm				
8:00 pm				
8:30 pm				

December LESSON PLANS   Week of 8th - 14th

	SUNDAY	MONDAY	TUESDAY	WEDNESDAY

THURSDAY	FRIDAY	SATURDAY

Weekly Supplies

☐ _____
☐ _____
☐ _____
☐ _____
☐ _____
☐ _____
☐ _____
☐ _____
☐ _____
☐ _____
☐ _____
☐ _____

To Dos

☐ _____
☐ _____
☐ _____
☐ _____
☐ _____
☐ _____
☐ _____
☐ _____
☐ _____
☐ _____
☐ _____

Notes

☐ _____
☐ _____
☐ _____
☐ _____
☐ _____
☐ _____
☐ _____
☐ _____
☐ _____

Weekly Schedule

	SUNDAY	MONDAY	TUESDAY
7:00 am			
7:30 am			
8:00 am			
8:30 am			
9:00 am			
9:30 am			
10:00 am			
10:30 am			
11:00 am			
11:30 am			
12:00 pm			
12:30 pm			
1:00 pm			
1:30 pm			
2:00 pm			
2:30 pm			
3:00 pm			
3:30 pm			
4:00 pm			
4:30 pm			
5:00 pm			
5:30 pm			
6:00 pm			
6:30 pm			
7:00 pm			
7:30 pm			
8:00 pm			
8:30 pm			

December

Week of 8th - 14th

	WEDNESDAY	THURSDAY	FRIDAY	SATURDAY
7:00 am				
7:30 am				
8:00 am				
8:30 am				
9:00 am				
9:30 am				
10:00 am				
10:30 am				
11:00 am				
11:30 am				
12:00 pm				
12:30 pm				
1:00 pm				
1:30 pm				
2:00 pm				
2:30 pm				
3:00 pm				
3:30 pm				
4:00 pm				
4:30 pm				
5:00 pm				
5:30 pm				
6:00 pm				
6:30 pm				
7:00 pm				
7:30 pm				
8:00 pm				
8:30 pm				

	SUNDAY	MONDAY	TUESDAY	WEDNESDAY

December LESSON PLANS Week of 15th - 21st

THURSDAY	FRIDAY	SATURDAY

Weekly Supplies

- ☐ _____
- ☐ _____
- ☐ _____
- ☐ _____
- ☐ _____
- ☐ _____
- ☐ _____
- ☐ _____
- ☐ _____
- ☐ _____
- ☐ _____
- ☐ _____

To Dos

- ☐ _____
- ☐ _____
- ☐ _____
- ☐ _____
- ☐ _____
- ☐ _____
- ☐ _____
- ☐ _____
- ☐ _____
- ☐ _____
- ☐ _____

Notes

- ☐ _____
- ☐ _____
- ☐ _____
- ☐ _____
- ☐ _____
- ☐ _____
- ☐ _____
- ☐ _____
- ☐ _____

Weekly Schedule

	SUNDAY	MONDAY	TUESDAY
7:00 am			
7:30 am			
8:00 am			
8:30 am			
9:00 am			
9:30 am			
10:00 am			
10:30 am			
11:00 am			
11:30 am			
12:00 pm			
12:30 pm			
1:00 pm			
1:30 pm			
2:00 pm			
2:30 pm			
3:00 pm			
3:30 pm			
4:00 pm			
4:30 pm			
5:00 pm			
5:30 pm			
6:00 pm			
6:30 pm			
7:00 pm			
7:30 pm			
8:00 pm			
8:30 pm			

December

Week of 15th - 21st

	WEDNESDAY	THURSDAY	FRIDAY	SATURDAY
7:00 am				
7:30 am				
8:00 am				
8:30 am				
9:00 am				
9:30 am				
10:00 am				
10:30 am				
11:00 am				
11:30 am				
12:00 pm				
12:30 pm				
1:00 pm				
1:30 pm				
2:00 pm				
2:30 pm				
3:00 pm				
3:30 pm				
4:00 pm				
4:30 pm				
5:00 pm				
5:30 pm				
6:00 pm				
6:30 pm				
7:00 pm				
7:30 pm				
8:00 pm				
8:30 pm				

	SUNDAY	MONDAY	TUESDAY	WEDNESDAY

December LESSON PLANS Week of 22nd - 28th

THURSDAY	FRIDAY	SATURDAY

Weekly Supplies

- ☐ _____
- ☐ _____
- ☐ _____
- ☐ _____
- ☐ _____
- ☐ _____
- ☐ _____
- ☐ _____
- ☐ _____
- ☐ _____
- ☐ _____
- ☐ _____

To Dos

- ☐ _____
- ☐ _____
- ☐ _____
- ☐ _____
- ☐ _____
- ☐ _____
- ☐ _____
- ☐ _____
- ☐ _____
- ☐ _____
- ☐ _____

Notes

- ☐ _____
- ☐ _____
- ☐ _____
- ☐ _____
- ☐ _____
- ☐ _____
- ☐ _____
- ☐ _____
- ☐ _____

Weekly Schedule

	SUNDAY	MONDAY	TUESDAY
7:00 am			
7:30 am			
8:00 am			
8:30 am			
9:00 am			
9:30 am			
10:00 am			
10:30 am			
11:00 am			
11:30 am			
12:00 pm			
12:30 pm			
1:00 pm			
1:30 pm			
2:00 pm			
2:30 pm			
3:00 pm			
3:30 pm			
4:00 pm			
4:30 pm			
5:00 pm			
5:30 pm			
6:00 pm			
6:30 pm			
7:00 pm			
7:30 pm			
8:00 pm			
8:30 pm			

December
Week of 22nd - 28th

	WEDNESDAY	THURSDAY	FRIDAY	SATURDAY
7:00 am				
7:30 am				
8:00 am				
8:30 am				
9:00 am				
9:30 am				
10:00 am				
10:30 am				
11:00 am				
11:30 am				
12:00 pm				
12:30 pm				
1:00 pm				
1:30 pm				
2:00 pm				
2:30 pm				
3:00 pm				
3:30 pm				
4:00 pm				
4:30 pm				
5:00 pm				
5:30 pm				
6:00 pm				
6:30 pm				
7:00 pm				
7:30 pm				
8:00 pm				
8:30 pm				

January 2025

SUNDAY	MONDAY	TUESDAY	WEDNESDAY
			1
5	6	7	8
12	13	14	15
19	20	21	22
26	27	28	29

THURSDAY	FRIDAY	SATURDAY	NOTES
2	3	4	
9	10	11	
16	17	18	
23	24	25	
30	31		

LESSON PLANS Week of 29th - 4th

Dec-Jan

	SUNDAY	MONDAY	TUESDAY	WEDNESDAY

	SUNDAY	MONDAY	TUESDAY	WEDNESDAY

THURSDAY	FRIDAY	SATURDAY

Weekly Supplies

☐ _____
☐ _____
☐ _____
☐ _____
☐ _____
☐ _____
☐ _____
☐ _____
☐ _____
☐ _____
☐ _____
☐ _____

To Dos

☐ _____
☐ _____
☐ _____
☐ _____
☐ _____
☐ _____
☐ _____
☐ _____
☐ _____
☐ _____
☐ _____

Notes

☐ _____
☐ _____
☐ _____
☐ _____
☐ _____
☐ _____
☐ _____
☐ _____
☐ _____

Weekly Schedule

	SUNDAY	MONDAY	TUESDAY
7:00 am			
7:30 am			
8:00 am			
8:30 am			
9:00 am			
9:30 am			
10:00 am			
10:30 am			
11:00 am			
11:30 am			
12:00 pm			
12:30 pm			
1:00 pm			
1:30 pm			
2:00 pm			
2:30 pm			
3:00 pm			
3:30 pm			
4:00 pm			
4:30 pm			
5:00 pm			
5:30 pm			
6:00 pm			
6:30 pm			
7:00 pm			
7:30 pm			
8:00 pm			
8:30 pm			

Dec-Jan

Week of 29th - 4th

	WEDNESDAY	THURSDAY	FRIDAY	SATURDAY
7:00 am				
7:30 am				
8:00 am				
8:30 am				
9:00 am				
9:30 am				
10:00 am				
10:30 am				
11:00 am				
11:30 am				
12:00 pm				
12:30 pm				
1:00 pm				
1:30 pm				
2:00 pm				
2:30 pm				
3:00 pm				
3:30 pm				
4:00 pm				
4:30 pm				
5:00 pm				
5:30 pm				
6:00 pm				
6:30 pm				
7:00 pm				
7:30 pm				
8:00 pm				
8:30 pm				

	SUNDAY	MONDAY	TUESDAY	WEDNESDAY

January LESSON PLANS Week of 5th - 11th

THURSDAY	FRIDAY	SATURDAY

Weekly Supplies

☐ _____
☐ _____
☐ _____
☐ _____
☐ _____
☐ _____
☐ _____
☐ _____
☐ _____
☐ _____
☐ _____
☐ _____

To Dos

☐ _____
☐ _____
☐ _____
☐ _____
☐ _____
☐ _____
☐ _____
☐ _____
☐ _____
☐ _____
☐ _____

Notes

☐ _____
☐ _____
☐ _____
☐ _____
☐ _____
☐ _____
☐ _____
☐ _____
☐ _____

Weekly Schedule

	SUNDAY	MONDAY	TUESDAY
7:00 am			
7:30 am			
8:00 am			
8:30 am			
9:00 am			
9:30 am			
10:00 am			
10:30 am			
11:00 am			
11:30 am			
12:00 pm			
12:30 pm			
1:00 pm			
1:30 pm			
2:00 pm			
2:30 pm			
3:00 pm			
3:30 pm			
4:00 pm			
4:30 pm			
5:00 pm			
5:30 pm			
6:00 pm			
6:30 pm			
7:00 pm			
7:30 pm			
8:00 pm			
8:30 pm			

January

Week of 5th - 11th

	WEDNESDAY	THURSDAY	FRIDAY	SATURDAY
7:00 am				
7:30 am				
8:00 am				
8:30 am				
9:00 am				
9:30 am				
10:00 am				
10:30 am				
11:00 am				
11:30 am				
12:00 pm				
12:30 pm				
1:00 pm				
1:30 pm				
2:00 pm				
2:30 pm				
3:00 pm				
3:30 pm				
4:00 pm				
4:30 pm				
5:00 pm				
5:30 pm				
6:00 pm				
6:30 pm				
7:00 pm				
7:30 pm				
8:00 pm				
8:30 pm				

	SUNDAY	MONDAY	TUESDAY	WEDNESDAY

January LESSON PLANS Week of 12th – 18th

	SUNDAY	MONDAY	TUESDAY	WEDNESDAY

THURSDAY	FRIDAY	SATURDAY

Weekly Supplies

☐ _____
☐ _____
☐ _____
☐ _____
☐ _____
☐ _____
☐ _____
☐ _____
☐ _____
☐ _____
☐ _____
☐ _____

To Dos

☐ _____
☐ _____
☐ _____
☐ _____
☐ _____
☐ _____
☐ _____
☐ _____
☐ _____
☐ _____
☐ _____

Notes

☐ _____
☐ _____
☐ _____
☐ _____
☐ _____
☐ _____
☐ _____
☐ _____
☐ _____

Weekly Schedule

	SUNDAY	MONDAY	TUESDAY
7:00 am			
7:30 am			
8:00 am			
8:30 am			
9:00 am			
9:30 am			
10:00 am			
10:30 am			
11:00 am			
11:30 am			
12:00 pm			
12:30 pm			
1:00 pm			
1:30 pm			
2:00 pm			
2:30 pm			
3:00 pm			
3:30 pm			
4:00 pm			
4:30 pm			
5:00 pm			
5:30 pm			
6:00 pm			
6:30 pm			
7:00 pm			
7:30 pm			
8:00 pm			
8:30 pm			

January
Week of 12th - 18th

	WEDNESDAY	THURSDAY	FRIDAY	SATURDAY
7:00 am				
7:30 am				
8:00 am				
8:30 am				
9:00 am				
9:30 am				
10:00 am				
10:30 am				
11:00 am				
11:30 am				
12:00 pm				
12:30 pm				
1:00 pm				
1:30 pm				
2:00 pm				
2:30 pm				
3:00 pm				
3:30 pm				
4:00 pm				
4:30 pm				
5:00 pm				
5:30 pm				
6:00 pm				
6:30 pm				
7:00 pm				
7:30 pm				
8:00 pm				
8:30 pm				

	SUNDAY	MONDAY	TUESDAY	WEDNESDAY

January LESSON PLANS Week of 19th - 25th

THURSDAY	FRIDAY	SATURDAY

Weekly Supplies

- ☐ _____
- ☐ _____
- ☐ _____
- ☐ _____
- ☐ _____
- ☐ _____
- ☐ _____
- ☐ _____
- ☐ _____
- ☐ _____
- ☐ _____
- ☐ _____

To Dos

- ☐ _____
- ☐ _____
- ☐ _____
- ☐ _____
- ☐ _____
- ☐ _____
- ☐ _____
- ☐ _____
- ☐ _____
- ☐ _____
- ☐ _____

Notes

- ☐ _____
- ☐ _____
- ☐ _____
- ☐ _____
- ☐ _____
- ☐ _____
- ☐ _____
- ☐ _____
- ☐ _____

Weekly Schedule

	SUNDAY	MONDAY	TUESDAY
7:00 am			
7:30 am			
8:00 am			
8:30 am			
9:00 am			
9:30 am			
10:00 am			
10:30 am			
11:00 am			
11:30 am			
12:00 pm			
12:30 pm			
1:00 pm			
1:30 pm			
2:00 pm			
2:30 pm			
3:00 pm			
3:30 pm			
4:00 pm			
4:30 pm			
5:00 pm			
5:30 pm			
6:00 pm			
6:30 pm			
7:00 pm			
7:30 pm			
8:00 pm			
8:30 pm			

January

Week of 19th - 25th

	WEDNESDAY	THURSDAY	FRIDAY	SATURDAY
7:00 am				
7:30 am				
8:00 am				
8:30 am				
9:00 am				
9:30 am				
10:00 am				
10:30 am				
11:00 am				
11:30 am				
12:00 pm				
12:30 pm				
1:00 pm				
1:30 pm				
2:00 pm				
2:30 pm				
3:00 pm				
3:30 pm				
4:00 pm				
4:30 pm				
5:00 pm				
5:30 pm				
6:00 pm				
6:30 pm				
7:00 pm				
7:30 pm				
8:00 pm				
8:30 pm				

	SUNDAY	MONDAY	TUESDAY	WEDNESDAY
	SUNDAY	MONDAY	TUESDAY	WEDNESDAY

Jan - Feb LESSON PLANS Week of 26th - 1st

THURSDAY	FRIDAY	SATURDAY

Weekly Supplies

- [ ] _____
- [ ] _____
- [ ] _____
- [ ] _____
- [ ] _____
- [ ] _____
- [ ] _____
- [ ] _____
- [ ] _____
- [ ] _____
- [ ] _____
- [ ] _____

To Dos

- [ ] _____
- [ ] _____
- [ ] _____
- [ ] _____
- [ ] _____
- [ ] _____
- [ ] _____
- [ ] _____
- [ ] _____
- [ ] _____
- [ ] _____
- [ ] _____

Notes

- [ ] _____
- [ ] _____
- [ ] _____
- [ ] _____
- [ ] _____
- [ ] _____
- [ ] _____
- [ ] _____
- [ ] _____

Weekly Schedule

	SUNDAY	MONDAY	TUESDAY
7:00 am			
7:30 am			
8:00 am			
8:30 am			
9:00 am			
9:30 am			
10:00 am			
10:30 am			
11:00 am			
11:30 am			
12:00 pm			
12:30 pm			
1:00 pm			
1:30 pm			
2:00 pm			
2:30 pm			
3:00 pm			
3:30 pm			
4:00 pm			
4:30 pm			
5:00 pm			
5:30 pm			
6:00 pm			
6:30 pm			
7:00 pm			
7:30 pm			
8:00 pm			
8:30 pm			

Jan -Feb Week of 26th - 1st

	WEDNESDAY	THURSDAY	FRIDAY	SATURDAY
7:00 am				
7:30 am				
8:00 am				
8:30 am				
9:00 am				
9:30 am				
10:00 am				
10:30 am				
11:00 am				
11:30 am				
12:00 pm				
12:30 pm				
1:00 pm				
1:30 pm				
2:00 pm				
2:30 pm				
3:00 pm				
3:30 pm				
4:00 pm				
4:30 pm				
5:00 pm				
5:30 pm				
6:00 pm				
6:30 pm				
7:00 pm				
7:30 pm				
8:00 pm				
8:30 pm				

February 2025

SUNDAY	MONDAY	TUESDAY	WEDNESDAY
2	3	4	5
9	10	11	12
16	17	18	19
23	24	25	26

THURSDAY	FRIDAY	SATURDAY	NOTES
		1	
6	7	8	
13	14	15	
20	21	22	
27	28		

February LESSON PLANS Week of 2nd - 8th

	SUNDAY	MONDAY	TUESDAY	WEDNESDAY

THURSDAY	FRIDAY	SATURDAY

Weekly Supplies

- [ ]
- [ ]
- [ ]
- [ ]
- [ ]
- [ ]
- [ ]
- [ ]
- [ ]
- [ ]
- [ ]
- [ ]

To Dos

- [ ]
- [ ]
- [ ]
- [ ]
- [ ]
- [ ]
- [ ]
- [ ]
- [ ]
- [ ]
- [ ]
- [ ]

Notes

- [ ]
- [ ]
- [ ]
- [ ]
- [ ]
- [ ]
- [ ]
- [ ]
- [ ]

Weekly Schedule

	SUNDAY	MONDAY	TUESDAY
7:00 am			
7:30 am			
8:00 am			
8:30 am			
9:00 am			
9:30 am			
10:00 am			
10:30 am			
11:00 am			
11:30 am			
12:00 pm			
12:30 pm			
1:00 pm			
1:30 pm			
2:00 pm			
2:30 pm			
3:00 pm			
3:30 pm			
4:00 pm			
4:30 pm			
5:00 pm			
5:30 pm			
6:00 pm			
6:30 pm			
7:00 pm			
7:30 pm			
8:00 pm			
8:30 pm			

February

Week of 2nd - 8th

	WEDNESDAY	THURSDAY	FRIDAY	SATURDAY
7:00 am				
7:30 am				
8:00 am				
8:30 am				
9:00 am				
9:30 am				
10:00 am				
10:30 am				
11:00 am				
11:30 am				
12:00 pm				
12:30 pm				
1:00 pm				
1:30 pm				
2:00 pm				
2:30 pm				
3:00 pm				
3:30 pm				
4:00 pm				
4:30 pm				
5:00 pm				
5:30 pm				
6:00 pm				
6:30 pm				
7:00 pm				
7:30 pm				
8:00 pm				
8:30 pm				

	SUNDAY	MONDAY	TUESDAY	WEDNESDAY

February LESSON PLANS Week of 9th – 15th

THURSDAY	FRIDAY	SATURDAY

Weekly Supplies

- [ ] _____
- [ ] _____
- [ ] _____
- [ ] _____
- [ ] _____
- [ ] _____
- [ ] _____
- [ ] _____
- [ ] _____
- [ ] _____
- [ ] _____
- [ ] _____

To Dos

- [ ] _____
- [ ] _____
- [ ] _____
- [ ] _____
- [ ] _____
- [ ] _____
- [ ] _____
- [ ] _____
- [ ] _____
- [ ] _____
- [ ] _____

Notes

- [ ] _____
- [ ] _____
- [ ] _____
- [ ] _____
- [ ] _____
- [ ] _____
- [ ] _____
- [ ] _____
- [ ] _____

Weekly Schedule

	SUNDAY	MONDAY	TUESDAY
7:00 am			
7:30 am			
8:00 am			
8:30 am			
9:00 am			
9:30 am			
10:00 am			
10:30 am			
11:00 am			
11:30 am			
12:00 pm			
12:30 pm			
1:00 pm			
1:30 pm			
2:00 pm			
2:30 pm			
3:00 pm			
3:30 pm			
4:00 pm			
4:30 pm			
5:00 pm			
5:30 pm			
6:00 pm			
6:30 pm			
7:00 pm			
7:30 pm			
8:00 pm			
8:30 pm			

February
Week of 9th - 15th

	WEDNESDAY	THURSDAY	FRIDAY	SATURDAY
7:00 am				
7:30 am				
8:00 am				
8:30 am				
9:00 am				
9:30 am				
10:00 am				
10:30 am				
11:00 am				
11:30 am				
12:00 pm				
12:30 pm				
1:00 pm				
1:30 pm				
2:00 pm				
2:30 pm				
3:00 pm				
3:30 pm				
4:00 pm				
4:30 pm				
5:00 pm				
5:30 pm				
6:00 pm				
6:30 pm				
7:00 pm				
7:30 pm				
8:00 pm				
8:30 pm				

	SUNDAY	MONDAY	TUESDAY	WEDNESDAY

February LESSON PLANS Week of 16th – 22nd

THURSDAY	FRIDAY	SATURDAY

Weekly Supplies

☐ _____
☐ _____
☐ _____
☐ _____
☐ _____
☐ _____
☐ _____
☐ _____
☐ _____
☐ _____
☐ _____
☐ _____

To Dos

☐ _____
☐ _____
☐ _____
☐ _____
☐ _____
☐ _____
☐ _____
☐ _____
☐ _____
☐ _____
☐ _____

Notes

☐ _____
☐ _____
☐ _____
☐ _____
☐ _____
☐ _____
☐ _____
☐ _____
☐ _____

Weekly Schedule

	SUNDAY	MONDAY	TUESDAY
7:00 am			
7:30 am			
8:00 am			
8:30 am			
9:00 am			
9:30 am			
10:00 am			
10:30 am			
11:00 am			
11:30 am			
12:00 pm			
12:30 pm			
1:00 pm			
1:30 pm			
2:00 pm			
2:30 pm			
3:00 pm			
3:30 pm			
4:00 pm			
4:30 pm			
5:00 pm			
5:30 pm			
6:00 pm			
6:30 pm			
7:00 pm			
7:30 pm			
8:00 pm			
8:30 pm			

February Week of 16th - 22nd

	WEDNESDAY	THURSDAY	FRIDAY	SATURDAY
7:00 am				
7:30 am				
8:00 am				
8:30 am				
9:00 am				
9:30 am				
10:00 am				
10:30 am				
11:00 am				
11:30 am				
12:00 pm				
12:30 pm				
1:00 pm				
1:30 pm				
2:00 pm				
2:30 pm				
3:00 pm				
3:30 pm				
4:00 pm				
4:30 pm				
5:00 pm				
5:30 pm				
6:00 pm				
6:30 pm				
7:00 pm				
7:30 pm				
8:00 pm				
8:30 pm				

	SUNDAY	MONDAY	TUESDAY	WEDNESDAY

Feb-Mar LESSON PLANS Week of 23rd - 1st

THURSDAY	FRIDAY	SATURDAY

Weekly Supplies

- ☐ _____
- ☐ _____
- ☐ _____
- ☐ _____
- ☐ _____
- ☐ _____
- ☐ _____
- ☐ _____
- ☐ _____
- ☐ _____
- ☐ _____
- ☐ _____

To Dos

- ☐ _____
- ☐ _____
- ☐ _____
- ☐ _____
- ☐ _____
- ☐ _____
- ☐ _____
- ☐ _____
- ☐ _____
- ☐ _____
- ☐ _____

Notes

- ☐ _____
- ☐ _____
- ☐ _____
- ☐ _____
- ☐ _____
- ☐ _____
- ☐ _____
- ☐ _____
- ☐ _____

Weekly Schedule

	SUNDAY	MONDAY	TUESDAY
7:00 am			
7:30 am			
8:00 am			
8:30 am			
9:00 am			
9:30 am			
10:00 am			
10:30 am			
11:00 am			
11:30 am			
12:00 pm			
12:30 pm			
1:00 pm			
1:30 pm			
2:00 pm			
2:30 pm			
3:00 pm			
3:30 pm			
4:00 pm			
4:30 pm			
5:00 pm			
5:30 pm			
6:00 pm			
6:30 pm			
7:00 pm			
7:30 pm			
8:00 pm			
8:30 pm			

Feb-Mar

Week of 23rd - 1st

	WEDNESDAY	THURSDAY	FRIDAY	SATURDAY
7:00 am				
7:30 am				
8:00 am				
8:30 am				
9:00 am				
9:30 am				
10:00 am				
10:30 am				
11:00 am				
11:30 am				
12:00 pm				
12:30 pm				
1:00 pm				
1:30 pm				
2:00 pm				
2:30 pm				
3:00 pm				
3:30 pm				
4:00 pm				
4:30 pm				
5:00 pm				
5:30 pm				
6:00 pm				
6:30 pm				
7:00 pm				
7:30 pm				
8:00 pm				
8:30 pm				

March 2025

SUNDAY	MONDAY	TUESDAY	WEDNESDAY
2	3	4	5
9	10	11	12
16	17	18	19
23	24	25	26
30	31		

THURSDAY	FRIDAY	SATURDAY	NOTES
		1	
6	7	8	
13	14	15	
20	21	22	
27	28	29	

March LESSON PLANS Week of 2nd - 8th

	SUNDAY	MONDAY	TUESDAY	WEDNESDAY

THURSDAY	FRIDAY	SATURDAY

Weekly Supplies

☐ _____
☐ _____
☐ _____
☐ _____
☐ _____
☐ _____
☐ _____
☐ _____
☐ _____
☐ _____
☐ _____
☐ _____

To Dos

☐ _____
☐ _____
☐ _____
☐ _____
☐ _____
☐ _____
☐ _____
☐ _____
☐ _____
☐ _____
☐ _____

Notes

☐ _____
☐ _____
☐ _____
☐ _____
☐ _____
☐ _____
☐ _____
☐ _____
☐ _____

Weekly Schedule

	SUNDAY	MONDAY	TUESDAY
7:00 am			
7:30 am			
8:00 am			
8:30 am			
9:00 am			
9:30 am			
10:00 am			
10:30 am			
11:00 am			
11:30 am			
12:00 pm			
12:30 pm			
1:00 pm			
1:30 pm			
2:00 pm			
2:30 pm			
3:00 pm			
3:30 pm			
4:00 pm			
4:30 pm			
5:00 pm			
5:30 pm			
6:00 pm			
6:30 pm			
7:00 pm			
7:30 pm			
8:00 pm			
8:30 pm			

March

Week of 2nd - 8th

	WEDNESDAY	THURSDAY	FRIDAY	SATURDAY
7:00 am				
7:30 am				
8:00 am				
8:30 am				
9:00 am				
9:30 am				
10:00 am				
10:30 am				
11:00 am				
11:30 am				
12:00 pm				
12:30 pm				
1:00 pm				
1:30 pm				
2:00 pm				
2:30 pm				
3:00 pm				
3:30 pm				
4:00 pm				
4:30 pm				
5:00 pm				
5:30 pm				
6:00 pm				
6:30 pm				
7:00 pm				
7:30 pm				
8:00 pm				
8:30 pm				

March

LESSON PLANS — Week of 9th – 15th

	SUNDAY	MONDAY	TUESDAY	WEDNESDAY

THURSDAY	FRIDAY	SATURDAY

Weekly Supplies

- ☐ _____
- ☐ _____
- ☐ _____
- ☐ _____
- ☐ _____
- ☐ _____
- ☐ _____
- ☐ _____
- ☐ _____
- ☐ _____
- ☐ _____
- ☐ _____

To Dos

- ☐ _____
- ☐ _____
- ☐ _____
- ☐ _____
- ☐ _____
- ☐ _____
- ☐ _____
- ☐ _____
- ☐ _____
- ☐ _____
- ☐ _____

Notes

- ☐ _____
- ☐ _____
- ☐ _____
- ☐ _____
- ☐ _____
- ☐ _____
- ☐ _____
- ☐ _____
- ☐ _____

Weekly Schedule

	SUNDAY	MONDAY	TUESDAY
7:00 am			
7:30 am			
8:00 am			
8:30 am			
9:00 am			
9:30 am			
10:00 am			
10:30 am			
11:00 am			
11:30 am			
12:00 pm			
12:30 pm			
1:00 pm			
1:30 pm			
2:00 pm			
2:30 pm			
3:00 pm			
3:30 pm			
4:00 pm			
4:30 pm			
5:00 pm			
5:30 pm			
6:00 pm			
6:30 pm			
7:00 pm			
7:30 pm			
8:00 pm			
8:30 pm			

March

Week of 9th - 15th

	WEDNESDAY	THURSDAY	FRIDAY	SATURDAY
7:00 am				
7:30 am				
8:00 am				
8:30 am				
9:00 am				
9:30 am				
10:00 am				
10:30 am				
11:00 am				
11:30 am				
12:00 pm				
12:30 pm				
1:00 pm				
1:30 pm				
2:00 pm				
2:30 pm				
3:00 pm				
3:30 pm				
4:00 pm				
4:30 pm				
5:00 pm				
5:30 pm				
6:00 pm				
6:30 pm				
7:00 pm				
7:30 pm				
8:00 pm				
8:30 pm				

March

LESSON PLANS   Week of 16th - 22nd

	SUNDAY	MONDAY	TUESDAY	WEDNESDAY

THURSDAY	FRIDAY	SATURDAY

Weekly Supplies

- ☐ ....
- ☐ ....
- ☐ ....
- ☐ ....
- ☐ ....
- ☐ ....
- ☐ ....
- ☐ ....
- ☐ ....
- ☐ ....
- ☐ ....
- ☐ ....

To Dos

- ☐ ....
- ☐ ....
- ☐ ....
- ☐ ....
- ☐ ....
- ☐ ....
- ☐ ....
- ☐ ....
- ☐ ....
- ☐ ....
- ☐ ....

Notes

- ☐ ....
- ☐ ....
- ☐ ....
- ☐ ....
- ☐ ....
- ☐ ....
- ☐ ....
- ☐ ....
- ☐ ....

Weekly Schedule

	SUNDAY	MONDAY	TUESDAY
7:00 am			
7:30 am			
8:00 am			
8:30 am			
9:00 am			
9:30 am			
10:00 am			
10:30 am			
11:00 am			
11:30 am			
12:00 pm			
12:30 pm			
1:00 pm			
1:30 pm			
2:00 pm			
2:30 pm			
3:00 pm			
3:30 pm			
4:00 pm			
4:30 pm			
5:00 pm			
5:30 pm			
6:00 pm			
6:30 pm			
7:00 pm			
7:30 pm			
8:00 pm			
8:30 pm			

March

Week of 16th - 22nd

	WEDNESDAY	THURSDAY	FRIDAY	SATURDAY
7:00 am				
7:30 am				
8:00 am				
8:30 am				
9:00 am				
9:30 am				
10:00 am				
10:30 am				
11:00 am				
11:30 am				
12:00 pm				
12:30 pm				
1:00 pm				
1:30 pm				
2:00 pm				
2:30 pm				
3:00 pm				
3:30 pm				
4:00 pm				
4:30 pm				
5:00 pm				
5:30 pm				
6:00 pm				
6:30 pm				
7:00 pm				
7:30 pm				
8:00 pm				
8:30 pm				

March

LESSON PLANS   Week of 23rd – 29th

	SUNDAY	MONDAY	TUESDAY	WEDNESDAY

THURSDAY	FRIDAY	SATURDAY

Weekly Supplies

- [ ] _____
- [ ] _____
- [ ] _____
- [ ] _____
- [ ] _____
- [ ] _____
- [ ] _____
- [ ] _____
- [ ] _____
- [ ] _____
- [ ] _____
- [ ] _____

To Dos

- [ ] _____
- [ ] _____
- [ ] _____
- [ ] _____
- [ ] _____
- [ ] _____
- [ ] _____
- [ ] _____
- [ ] _____
- [ ] _____
- [ ] _____

Notes

- [ ] _____
- [ ] _____
- [ ] _____
- [ ] _____
- [ ] _____
- [ ] _____
- [ ] _____
- [ ] _____
- [ ] _____

Weekly Schedule

	SUNDAY	MONDAY	TUESDAY
7:00 am			
7:30 am			
8:00 am			
8:30 am			
9:00 am			
9:30 am			
10:00 am			
10:30 am			
11:00 am			
11:30 am			
12:00 pm			
12:30 pm			
1:00 pm			
1:30 pm			
2:00 pm			
2:30 pm			
3:00 pm			
3:30 pm			
4:00 pm			
4:30 pm			
5:00 pm			
5:30 pm			
6:00 pm			
6:30 pm			
7:00 pm			
7:30 pm			
8:00 pm			
8:30 pm			

March

Week of 23rd - 29th

	WEDNESDAY	THURSDAY	FRIDAY	SATURDAY
7:00 am				
7:30 am				
8:00 am				
8:30 am				
9:00 am				
9:30 am				
10:00 am				
10:30 am				
11:00 am				
11:30 am				
12:00 pm				
12:30 pm				
1:00 pm				
1:30 pm				
2:00 pm				
2:30 pm				
3:00 pm				
3:30 pm				
4:00 pm				
4:30 pm				
5:00 pm				
5:30 pm				
6:00 pm				
6:30 pm				
7:00 pm				
7:30 pm				
8:00 pm				
8:30 pm				

April 2025

SUNDAY	MONDAY	TUESDAY	WEDNESDAY
		1	2
6	7	8	9
13	14	15	16
20	21	22	23
27	28	29	30

THURSDAY	FRIDAY	SATURDAY	NOTES
3	4	5	
10	11	12	
17	18	19	
24	25	26	

Mar-Apr LESSON PLANS   Week of 30th - 5th

SUNDAY	MONDAY	TUESDAY	WEDNESDAY

THURSDAY	FRIDAY	SATURDAY

Weekly Supplies

- ☐ _____
- ☐ _____
- ☐ _____
- ☐ _____
- ☐ _____
- ☐ _____
- ☐ _____
- ☐ _____
- ☐ _____
- ☐ _____
- ☐ _____
- ☐ _____

To Dos

- ☐ _____
- ☐ _____
- ☐ _____
- ☐ _____
- ☐ _____
- ☐ _____
- ☐ _____
- ☐ _____
- ☐ _____
- ☐ _____
- ☐ _____

Notes

- ☐ _____
- ☐ _____
- ☐ _____
- ☐ _____
- ☐ _____
- ☐ _____
- ☐ _____
- ☐ _____
- ☐ _____

Weekly Schedule

	SUNDAY	MONDAY	TUESDAY
7:00 am			
7:30 am			
8:00 am			
8:30 am			
9:00 am			
9:30 am			
10:00 am			
10:30 am			
11:00 am			
11:30 am			
12:00 pm			
12:30 pm			
1:00 pm			
1:30 pm			
2:00 pm			
2:30 pm			
3:00 pm			
3:30 pm			
4:00 pm			
4:30 pm			
5:00 pm			
5:30 pm			
6:00 pm			
6:30 pm			
7:00 pm			
7:30 pm			
8:00 pm			
8:30 pm			

Mar-Apr

Week of 30th - 5th

	WEDNESDAY	THURSDAY	FRIDAY	SATURDAY
7:00 am				
7:30 am				
8:00 am				
8:30 am				
9:00 am				
9:30 am				
10:00 am				
10:30 am				
11:00 am				
11:30 am				
12:00 pm				
12:30 pm				
1:00 pm				
1:30 pm				
2:00 pm				
2:30 pm				
3:00 pm				
3:30 pm				
4:00 pm				
4:30 pm				
5:00 pm				
5:30 pm				
6:00 pm				
6:30 pm				
7:00 pm				
7:30 pm				
8:00 pm				
8:30 pm				

April LESSON PLANS Week of 6th - 12th

	SUNDAY	MONDAY	TUESDAY	WEDNESDAY

THURSDAY	FRIDAY	SATURDAY

Weekly Supplies

- ☐ _____
- ☐ _____
- ☐ _____
- ☐ _____
- ☐ _____
- ☐ _____
- ☐ _____
- ☐ _____
- ☐ _____
- ☐ _____
- ☐ _____
- ☐ _____

To Dos

- ☐ _____
- ☐ _____
- ☐ _____
- ☐ _____
- ☐ _____
- ☐ _____
- ☐ _____
- ☐ _____
- ☐ _____
- ☐ _____
- ☐ _____

Notes

- ☐ _____
- ☐ _____
- ☐ _____
- ☐ _____
- ☐ _____
- ☐ _____
- ☐ _____
- ☐ _____
- ☐ _____

Weekly Schedule

	SUNDAY	MONDAY	TUESDAY
7:00 am			
7:30 am			
8:00 am			
8:30 am			
9:00 am			
9:30 am			
10:00 am			
10:30 am			
11:00 am			
11:30 am			
12:00 pm			
12:30 pm			
1:00 pm			
1:30 pm			
2:00 pm			
2:30 pm			
3:00 pm			
3:30 pm			
4:00 pm			
4:30 pm			
5:00 pm			
5:30 pm			
6:00 pm			
6:30 pm			
7:00 pm			
7:30 pm			
8:00 pm			
8:30 pm			

April

Week of 6th - 12th

	WEDNESDAY	THURSDAY	FRIDAY	SATURDAY
7:00 am				
7:30 am				
8:00 am				
8:30 am				
9:00 am				
9:30 am				
10:00 am				
10:30 am				
11:00 am				
11:30 am				
12:00 pm				
12:30 pm				
1:00 pm				
1:30 pm				
2:00 pm				
2:30 pm				
3:00 pm				
3:30 pm				
4:00 pm				
4:30 pm				
5:00 pm				
5:30 pm				
6:00 pm				
6:30 pm				
7:00 pm				
7:30 pm				
8:00 pm				
8:30 pm				

	SUNDAY	MONDAY	TUESDAY	WEDNESDAY

April LESSON PLANS Week of 13th - 19th

THURSDAY	FRIDAY	SATURDAY

Weekly Supplies

☐ _____
☐ _____
☐ _____
☐ _____
☐ _____
☐ _____
☐ _____
☐ _____
☐ _____
☐ _____
☐ _____
☐ _____

To Dos

☐ _____
☐ _____
☐ _____
☐ _____
☐ _____
☐ _____
☐ _____
☐ _____
☐ _____
☐ _____
☐ _____
☐ _____

Notes

☐ _____
☐ _____
☐ _____
☐ _____
☐ _____
☐ _____
☐ _____
☐ _____
☐ _____

Weekly Schedule

	SUNDAY	MONDAY	TUESDAY
7:00 am			
7:30 am			
8:00 am			
8:30 am			
9:00 am			
9:30 am			
10:00 am			
10:30 am			
11:00 am			
11:30 am			
12:00 pm			
12:30 pm			
1:00 pm			
1:30 pm			
2:00 pm			
2:30 pm			
3:00 pm			
3:30 pm			
4:00 pm			
4:30 pm			
5:00 pm			
5:30 pm			
6:00 pm			
6:30 pm			
7:00 pm			
7:30 pm			
8:00 pm			
8:30 pm			

April

Week of 13th - 19th

	WEDNESDAY	THURSDAY	FRIDAY	SATURDAY
7:00 am				
7:30 am				
8:00 am				
8:30 am				
9:00 am				
9:30 am				
10:00 am				
10:30 am				
11:00 am				
11:30 am				
12:00 pm				
12:30 pm				
1:00 pm				
1:30 pm				
2:00 pm				
2:30 pm				
3:00 pm				
3:30 pm				
4:00 pm				
4:30 pm				
5:00 pm				
5:30 pm				
6:00 pm				
6:30 pm				
7:00 pm				
7:30 pm				
8:00 pm				
8:30 pm				

April LESSON PLANS   Week of 20th - 26th

	SUNDAY	MONDAY	TUESDAY	WEDNESDAY

THURSDAY	FRIDAY	SATURDAY

Weekly Supplies

- [ ] _____
- [ ] _____
- [ ] _____
- [ ] _____
- [ ] _____
- [ ] _____
- [ ] _____
- [ ] _____
- [ ] _____
- [ ] _____
- [ ] _____
- [ ] _____

To Dos

- [ ] _____
- [ ] _____
- [ ] _____
- [ ] _____
- [ ] _____
- [ ] _____
- [ ] _____
- [ ] _____
- [ ] _____
- [ ] _____
- [ ] _____

Notes

- [ ] _____
- [ ] _____
- [ ] _____
- [ ] _____
- [ ] _____
- [ ] _____
- [ ] _____
- [ ] _____
- [ ] _____

Weekly Schedule

	SUNDAY	MONDAY	TUESDAY
7:00 am			
7:30 am			
8:00 am			
8:30 am			
9:00 am			
9:30 am			
10:00 am			
10:30 am			
11:00 am			
11:30 am			
12:00 pm			
12:30 pm			
1:00 pm			
1:30 pm			
2:00 pm			
2:30 pm			
3:00 pm			
3:30 pm			
4:00 pm			
4:30 pm			
5:00 pm			
5:30 pm			
6:00 pm			
6:30 pm			
7:00 pm			
7:30 pm			
8:00 pm			
8:30 pm			

April

Week of 20th - 26th

	WEDNESDAY	THURSDAY	FRIDAY	SATURDAY
7:00 am				
7:30 am				
8:00 am				
8:30 am				
9:00 am				
9:30 am				
10:00 am				
10:30 am				
11:00 am				
11:30 am				
12:00 pm				
12:30 pm				
1:00 pm				
1:30 pm				
2:00 pm				
2:30 pm				
3:00 pm				
3:30 pm				
4:00 pm				
4:30 pm				
5:00 pm				
5:30 pm				
6:00 pm				
6:30 pm				
7:00 pm				
7:30 pm				
8:00 pm				
8:30 pm				

	SUNDAY	MONDAY	TUESDAY	WEDNESDAY

THURSDAY	FRIDAY	SATURDAY

- ☐ _____
- ☐ _____
- ☐ _____
- ☐ _____
- ☐ _____
- ☐ _____
- ☐ _____
- ☐ _____
- ☐ _____
- ☐ _____
- ☐ _____
- ☐ _____

To Dos

- ☐ _____
- ☐ _____
- ☐ _____
- ☐ _____
- ☐ _____
- ☐ _____
- ☐ _____
- ☐ _____
- ☐ _____
- ☐ _____
- ☐ _____

Notes

- ☐ _____
- ☐ _____
- ☐ _____
- ☐ _____
- ☐ _____
- ☐ _____
- ☐ _____
- ☐ _____
- ☐ _____

Weekly Schedule

	SUNDAY	MONDAY	TUESDAY
7:00 am			
7:30 am			
8:00 am			
8:30 am			
9:00 am			
9:30 am			
10:00 am			
10:30 am			
11:00 am			
11:30 am			
12:00 pm			
12:30 pm			
1:00 pm			
1:30 pm			
2:00 pm			
2:30 pm			
3:00 pm			
3:30 pm			
4:00 pm			
4:30 pm			
5:00 pm			
5:30 pm			
6:00 pm			
6:30 pm			
7:00 pm			
7:30 pm			
8:00 pm			
8:30 pm			

Apr-May
Week of 27th - 3rd

	WEDNESDAY	THURSDAY	FRIDAY	SATURDAY
7:00 am				
7:30 am				
8:00 am				
8:30 am				
9:00 am				
9:30 am				
10:00 am				
10:30 am				
11:00 am				
11:30 am				
12:00 pm				
12:30 pm				
1:00 pm				
1:30 pm				
2:00 pm				
2:30 pm				
3:00 pm				
3:30 pm				
4:00 pm				
4:30 pm				
5:00 pm				
5:30 pm				
6:00 pm				
6:30 pm				
7:00 pm				
7:30 pm				
8:00 pm				
8:30 pm				

May 2025

SUNDAY	MONDAY	TUESDAY	WEDNESDAY
4	5	6	7
11	12	13	14
18	19	20	21
25	26	27	28

THURSDAY	FRIDAY	SATURDAY	NOTES
1	2	3	
8	9	10	
15	16	17	
22	23	24	
29	30	31	

	SUNDAY	MONDAY	TUESDAY	WEDNESDAY

May LESSON PLANS Week of 4th - 10th

| | SUNDAY | MONDAY | TUESDAY | WEDNESDAY |

THURSDAY	FRIDAY	SATURDAY

Weekly Supplies

- ☐ _____
- ☐ _____
- ☐ _____
- ☐ _____
- ☐ _____
- ☐ _____
- ☐ _____
- ☐ _____
- ☐ _____
- ☐ _____
- ☐ _____
- ☐ _____

To Dos

- ☐ _____
- ☐ _____
- ☐ _____
- ☐ _____
- ☐ _____
- ☐ _____
- ☐ _____
- ☐ _____
- ☐ _____
- ☐ _____
- ☐ _____
- ☐ _____

Notes

- ☐ _____
- ☐ _____
- ☐ _____
- ☐ _____
- ☐ _____
- ☐ _____
- ☐ _____
- ☐ _____
- ☐ _____

Weekly Schedule

	SUNDAY	MONDAY	TUESDAY
7:00 am			
7:30 am			
8:00 am			
8:30 am			
9:00 am			
9:30 am			
10:00 am			
10:30 am			
11:00 am			
11:30 am			
12:00 pm			
12:30 pm			
1:00 pm			
1:30 pm			
2:00 pm			
2:30 pm			
3:00 pm			
3:30 pm			
4:00 pm			
4:30 pm			
5:00 pm			
5:30 pm			
6:00 pm			
6:30 pm			
7:00 pm			
7:30 pm			
8:00 pm			
8:30 pm			

May

Week of 4th - 10th

	WEDNESDAY	THURSDAY	FRIDAY	SATURDAY
7:00 am				
7:30 am				
8:00 am				
8:30 am				
9:00 am				
9:30 am				
10:00 am				
10:30 am				
11:00 am				
11:30 am				
12:00 pm				
12:30 pm				
1:00 pm				
1:30 pm				
2:00 pm				
2:30 pm				
3:00 pm				
3:30 pm				
4:00 pm				
4:30 pm				
5:00 pm				
5:30 pm				
6:00 pm				
6:30 pm				
7:00 pm				
7:30 pm				
8:00 pm				
8:30 pm				

	SUNDAY	MONDAY	TUESDAY	WEDNESDAY

May LESSON PLANS Week of 11th – 17th

THURSDAY	FRIDAY	SATURDAY

- ☐ _____
- ☐ _____
- ☐ _____
- ☐ _____
- ☐ _____
- ☐ _____
- ☐ _____
- ☐ _____
- ☐ _____
- ☐ _____
- ☐ _____
- ☐ _____

To Dos

- ☐ _____
- ☐ _____
- ☐ _____
- ☐ _____
- ☐ _____
- ☐ _____
- ☐ _____
- ☐ _____
- ☐ _____
- ☐ _____
- ☐ _____
- ☐ _____

Notes

- ☐ _____
- ☐ _____
- ☐ _____
- ☐ _____
- ☐ _____
- ☐ _____
- ☐ _____
- ☐ _____
- ☐ _____

Weekly Schedule

	SUNDAY	MONDAY	TUESDAY
7:00 am			
7:30 am			
8:00 am			
8:30 am			
9:00 am			
9:30 am			
10:00 am			
10:30 am			
11:00 am			
11:30 am			
12:00 pm			
12:30 pm			
1:00 pm			
1:30 pm			
2:00 pm			
2:30 pm			
3:00 pm			
3:30 pm			
4:00 pm			
4:30 pm			
5:00 pm			
5:30 pm			
6:00 pm			
6:30 pm			
7:00 pm			
7:30 pm			
8:00 pm			
8:30 pm			

May

Week of 11th - 17th

	WEDNESDAY	THURSDAY	FRIDAY	SATURDAY
7:00 am				
7:30 am				
8:00 am				
8:30 am				
9:00 am				
9:30 am				
10:00 am				
10:30 am				
11:00 am				
11:30 am				
12:00 pm				
12:30 pm				
1:00 pm				
1:30 pm				
2:00 pm				
2:30 pm				
3:00 pm				
3:30 pm				
4:00 pm				
4:30 pm				
5:00 pm				
5:30 pm				
6:00 pm				
6:30 pm				
7:00 pm				
7:30 pm				
8:00 pm				
8:30 pm				

	SUNDAY	MONDAY	TUESDAY	WEDNESDAY

May LESSON PLANS Week of 18th - 24th

THURSDAY	FRIDAY	SATURDAY

Weekly Supplies

- ☐ _____
- ☐ _____
- ☐ _____
- ☐ _____
- ☐ _____
- ☐ _____
- ☐ _____
- ☐ _____
- ☐ _____
- ☐ _____
- ☐ _____
- ☐ _____

To Dos

- ☐ _____
- ☐ _____
- ☐ _____
- ☐ _____
- ☐ _____
- ☐ _____
- ☐ _____
- ☐ _____
- ☐ _____
- ☐ _____
- ☐ _____

Notes

- ☐ _____
- ☐ _____
- ☐ _____
- ☐ _____
- ☐ _____
- ☐ _____
- ☐ _____
- ☐ _____
- ☐ _____

Weekly Schedule

	SUNDAY	MONDAY	TUESDAY
7:00 am			
7:30 am			
8:00 am			
8:30 am			
9:00 am			
9:30 am			
10:00 am			
10:30 am			
11:00 am			
11:30 am			
12:00 pm			
12:30 pm			
1:00 pm			
1:30 pm			
2:00 pm			
2:30 pm			
3:00 pm			
3:30 pm			
4:00 pm			
4:30 pm			
5:00 pm			
5:30 pm			
6:00 pm			
6:30 pm			
7:00 pm			
7:30 pm			
8:00 pm			
8:30 pm			

May

Week of 18th - 24th

	WEDNESDAY	THURSDAY	FRIDAY	SATURDAY
7:00 am				
7:30 am				
8:00 am				
8:30 am				
9:00 am				
9:30 am				
10:00 am				
10:30 am				
11:00 am				
11:30 am				
12:00 pm				
12:30 pm				
1:00 pm				
1:30 pm				
2:00 pm				
2:30 pm				
3:00 pm				
3:30 pm				
4:00 pm				
4:30 pm				
5:00 pm				
5:30 pm				
6:00 pm				
6:30 pm				
7:00 pm				
7:30 pm				
8:00 pm				
8:30 pm				

May LESSON PLANS Week of 25th - 31st

	SUNDAY	MONDAY	TUESDAY	WEDNESDAY

THURSDAY	FRIDAY	SATURDAY

Weekly Supplies

- [ ] _____
- [ ] _____
- [ ] _____
- [ ] _____
- [ ] _____
- [ ] _____
- [ ] _____
- [ ] _____
- [ ] _____
- [ ] _____
- [ ] _____
- [ ] _____

To Dos

- [ ] _____
- [ ] _____
- [ ] _____
- [ ] _____
- [ ] _____
- [ ] _____
- [ ] _____
- [ ] _____
- [ ] _____
- [ ] _____
- [ ] _____
- [ ] _____

Notes

- [ ] _____
- [ ] _____
- [ ] _____
- [ ] _____
- [ ] _____
- [ ] _____
- [ ] _____
- [ ] _____
- [ ] _____

Weekly Schedule

	SUNDAY	MONDAY	TUESDAY
7:00 am			
7:30 am			
8:00 am			
8:30 am			
9:00 am			
9:30 am			
10:00 am			
10:30 am			
11:00 am			
11:30 am			
12:00 pm			
12:30 pm			
1:00 pm			
1:30 pm			
2:00 pm			
2:30 pm			
3:00 pm			
3:30 pm			
4:00 pm			
4:30 pm			
5:00 pm			
5:30 pm			
6:00 pm			
6:30 pm			
7:00 pm			
7:30 pm			
8:00 pm			
8:30 pm			

May

Week of 25th - 31st

	WEDNESDAY	THURSDAY	FRIDAY	SATURDAY
7:00 am				
7:30 am				
8:00 am				
8:30 am				
9:00 am				
9:30 am				
10:00 am				
10:30 am				
11:00 am				
11:30 am				
12:00 pm				
12:30 pm				
1:00 pm				
1:30 pm				
2:00 pm				
2:30 pm				
3:00 pm				
3:30 pm				
4:00 pm				
4:30 pm				
5:00 pm				
5:30 pm				
6:00 pm				
6:30 pm				
7:00 pm				
7:30 pm				
8:00 pm				
8:30 pm				

June 2025

SUNDAY	MONDAY	TUESDAY	WEDNESDAY
1	2	3	4
8	9	10	11
15	16	17	18
22	23	24	25
29	30		

THURSDAY	FRIDAY	SATURDAY	NOTES
5	6	7	
12	13	14	
19	20	21	
26	27	28	

	SUNDAY	MONDAY	TUESDAY	WEDNESDAY

June LESSON PLANS Week of 1st – 7th

THURSDAY	FRIDAY	SATURDAY

Weekly Supplies

☐ _____
☐ _____
☐ _____
☐ _____
☐ _____
☐ _____
☐ _____
☐ _____
☐ _____
☐ _____
☐ _____
☐ _____

To Dos

☐ _____
☐ _____
☐ _____
☐ _____
☐ _____
☐ _____
☐ _____
☐ _____
☐ _____
☐ _____
☐ _____

Notes

☐ _____
☐ _____
☐ _____
☐ _____
☐ _____
☐ _____
☐ _____
☐ _____
☐ _____

Weekly Schedule

	SUNDAY	MONDAY	TUESDAY
7:00 am			
7:30 am			
8:00 am			
8:30 am			
9:00 am			
9:30 am			
10:00 am			
10:30 am			
11:00 am			
11:30 am			
12:00 pm			
12:30 pm			
1:00 pm			
1:30 pm			
2:00 pm			
2:30 pm			
3:00 pm			
3:30 pm			
4:00 pm			
4:30 pm			
5:00 pm			
5:30 pm			
6:00 pm			
6:30 pm			
7:00 pm			
7:30 pm			
8:00 pm			
8:30 pm			

June

Week of 1st -7th

	WEDNESDAY	THURSDAY	FRIDAY	SATURDAY
7:00 am				
7:30 am				
8:00 am				
8:30 am				
9:00 am				
9:30 am				
10:00 am				
10:30 am				
11:00 am				
11:30 am				
12:00 pm				
12:30 pm				
1:00 pm				
1:30 pm				
2:00 pm				
2:30 pm				
3:00 pm				
3:30 pm				
4:00 pm				
4:30 pm				
5:00 pm				
5:30 pm				
6:00 pm				
6:30 pm				
7:00 pm				
7:30 pm				
8:00 pm				
8:30 pm				

	SUNDAY	MONDAY	TUESDAY	WEDNESDAY

June LESSON PLANS Week of 8th - 14th

THURSDAY	FRIDAY	SATURDAY

Weekly Supplies

☐ _____
☐ _____
☐ _____
☐ _____
☐ _____
☐ _____
☐ _____
☐ _____
☐ _____
☐ _____
☐ _____
☐ _____

To Dos

☐ _____
☐ _____
☐ _____
☐ _____
☐ _____
☐ _____
☐ _____
☐ _____
☐ _____
☐ _____
☐ _____
☐ _____

Notes

☐ _____
☐ _____
☐ _____
☐ _____
☐ _____
☐ _____
☐ _____
☐ _____
☐ _____

Weekly Schedule

	SUNDAY	MONDAY	TUESDAY
7:00 am			
7:30 am			
8:00 am			
8:30 am			
9:00 am			
9:30 am			
10:00 am			
10:30 am			
11:00 am			
11:30 am			
12:00 pm			
12:30 pm			
1:00 pm			
1:30 pm			
2:00 pm			
2:30 pm			
3:00 pm			
3:30 pm			
4:00 pm			
4:30 pm			
5:00 pm			
5:30 pm			
6:00 pm			
6:30 pm			
7:00 pm			
7:30 pm			
8:00 pm			
8:30 pm			

June

Week of 8th - 14th

	WEDNESDAY	THURSDAY	FRIDAY	SATURDAY
7:00 am				
7:30 am				
8:00 am				
8:30 am				
9:00 am				
9:30 am				
10:00 am				
10:30 am				
11:00 am				
11:30 am				
12:00 pm				
12:30 pm				
1:00 pm				
1:30 pm				
2:00 pm				
2:30 pm				
3:00 pm				
3:30 pm				
4:00 pm				
4:30 pm				
5:00 pm				
5:30 pm				
6:00 pm				
6:30 pm				
7:00 pm				
7:30 pm				
8:00 pm				
8:30 pm				

	SUNDAY	MONDAY	TUESDAY	WEDNESDAY

June LESSON PLANS Week of 15th – 21st

THURSDAY	FRIDAY	SATURDAY

Weekly Supplies

☐ _____
☐ _____
☐ _____
☐ _____
☐ _____
☐ _____
☐ _____
☐ _____
☐ _____
☐ _____
☐ _____
☐ _____

To Dos

☐ _____
☐ _____
☐ _____
☐ _____
☐ _____
☐ _____
☐ _____
☐ _____
☐ _____
☐ _____
☐ _____

Notes

☐ _____
☐ _____
☐ _____
☐ _____
☐ _____
☐ _____
☐ _____
☐ _____
☐ _____

Weekly Schedule

	SUNDAY	MONDAY	TUESDAY
7:00 am			
7:30 am			
8:00 am			
8:30 am			
9:00 am			
9:30 am			
10:00 am			
10:30 am			
11:00 am			
11:30 am			
12:00 pm			
12:30 pm			
1:00 pm			
1:30 pm			
2:00 pm			
2:30 pm			
3:00 pm			
3:30 pm			
4:00 pm			
4:30 pm			
5:00 pm			
5:30 pm			
6:00 pm			
6:30 pm			
7:00 pm			
7:30 pm			
8:00 pm			
8:30 pm			

June

Week of 15th - 21st

	WEDNESDAY	THURSDAY	FRIDAY	SATURDAY
7:00 am				
7:30 am				
8:00 am				
8:30 am				
9:00 am				
9:30 am				
10:00 am				
10:30 am				
11:00 am				
11:30 am				
12:00 pm				
12:30 pm				
1:00 pm				
1:30 pm				
2:00 pm				
2:30 pm				
3:00 pm				
3:30 pm				
4:00 pm				
4:30 pm				
5:00 pm				
5:30 pm				
6:00 pm				
6:30 pm				
7:00 pm				
7:30 pm				
8:00 pm				
8:30 pm				

June LESSON PLANS Week of 22nd - 28th

	SUNDAY	MONDAY	TUESDAY	WEDNESDAY

THURSDAY	FRIDAY	SATURDAY

Weekly Supplies

☐ _____
☐ _____
☐ _____
☐ _____
☐ _____
☐ _____
☐ _____
☐ _____
☐ _____
☐ _____
☐ _____
☐ _____

To Dos

☐ _____
☐ _____
☐ _____
☐ _____
☐ _____
☐ _____
☐ _____
☐ _____
☐ _____
☐ _____
☐ _____

Notes

☐ _____
☐ _____
☐ _____
☐ _____
☐ _____
☐ _____
☐ _____
☐ _____
☐ _____

Weekly Schedule

	SUNDAY	MONDAY	TUESDAY
7:00 am			
7:30 am			
8:00 am			
8:30 am			
9:00 am			
9:30 am			
10:00 am			
10:30 am			
11:00 am			
11:30 am			
12:00 pm			
12:30 pm			
1:00 pm			
1:30 pm			
2:00 pm			
2:30 pm			
3:00 pm			
3:30 pm			
4:00 pm			
4:30 pm			
5:00 pm			
5:30 pm			
6:00 pm			
6:30 pm			
7:00 pm			
7:30 pm			
8:00 pm			
8:30 pm			

June

Week of 22nd - 28th

	WEDNESDAY	THURSDAY	FRIDAY	SATURDAY
7:00 am				
7:30 am				
8:00 am				
8:30 am				
9:00 am				
9:30 am				
10:00 am				
10:30 am				
11:00 am				
11:30 am				
12:00 pm				
12:30 pm				
1:00 pm				
1:30 pm				
2:00 pm				
2:30 pm				
3:00 pm				
3:30 pm				
4:00 pm				
4:30 pm				
5:00 pm				
5:30 pm				
6:00 pm				
6:30 pm				
7:00 pm				
7:30 pm				
8:00 pm				
8:30 pm				

	SUNDAY	MONDAY	TUESDAY	WEDNESDAY

Jun-Jul LESSON PLANS Week of 29th - 5th

THURSDAY	FRIDAY	SATURDAY

Weekly Supplies

- [ ] _____
- [ ] _____
- [ ] _____
- [ ] _____
- [ ] _____
- [ ] _____
- [ ] _____
- [ ] _____
- [ ] _____
- [ ] _____
- [ ] _____
- [ ] _____

To Dos

- [ ] _____
- [ ] _____
- [ ] _____
- [ ] _____
- [ ] _____
- [ ] _____
- [ ] _____
- [ ] _____
- [ ] _____
- [ ] _____
- [ ] _____

Notes

- [ ] _____
- [ ] _____
- [ ] _____
- [ ] _____
- [ ] _____
- [ ] _____
- [ ] _____
- [ ] _____
- [ ] _____

Weekly Schedule

	SUNDAY	MONDAY	TUESDAY
7:00 am			
7:30 am			
8:00 am			
8:30 am			
9:00 am			
9:30 am			
10:00 am			
10:30 am			
11:00 am			
11:30 am			
12:00 pm			
12:30 pm			
1:00 pm			
1:30 pm			
2:00 pm			
2:30 pm			
3:00 pm			
3:30 pm			
4:00 pm			
4:30 pm			
5:00 pm			
5:30 pm			
6:00 pm			
6:30 pm			
7:00 pm			
7:30 pm			
8:00 pm			
8:30 pm			

Jun-Jul Week of 29th - 5th

	WEDNESDAY	THURSDAY	FRIDAY	SATURDAY
7:00 am				
7:30 am				
8:00 am				
8:30 am				
9:00 am				
9:30 am				
10:00 am				
10:30 am				
11:00 am				
11:30 am				
12:00 pm				
12:30 pm				
1:00 pm				
1:30 pm				
2:00 pm				
2:30 pm				
3:00 pm				
3:30 pm				
4:00 pm				
4:30 pm				
5:00 pm				
5:30 pm				
6:00 pm				
6:30 pm				
7:00 pm				
7:30 pm				
8:00 pm				
8:30 pm				

THANK YOU FOR PURCHASING MY HOMESCHOOL PLANNER!

I APPRECIATE YOU SUPPORTING MY SMALL BUSINESS.

PLEASE FEEL FREE TO LEAVE AN HONEST REVIEW ON AMAZON.

Made in the USA
Monee, IL
12 September 2024

65617598R00144